THE C●NFIDENCE BREAKTHROUGH

JO BLAKELEY

Published in 2025 by Mijoma Books

Copyright © Jo Blakely 2025

Jo Blakeley has asserted her right to be identified as the author of this Work in accordance with the Copyright, Designs and Patents Act 1988

ISBN Paperback: 978-0-9957305-2-6
Ebook: 978-0-9957305-3-3

All rights reserved. No part of this publication may be reproduced, stored in a retrieval system, or transmitted in any form or by any means, electronic, mechanical, photocopying, recording or otherwise, without the prior permission of the copyright owner.

Photos from Pixabay: Thanks to F1Digital; Tumisu; Wikimedia Images; Peterisurtans

A CIP catalogue copy of this book can be found in the British Library.

Published with the help of Indie Authors World
www.indieauthorsworld.com

IndieAuthors World

To my wonderful husband and our gorgeous son:
I love you both to the moon and back infinity.

Contents

ABOUT THE BOOK	9
MEET SAM	11
PART ONE - UNDERSTANDING THE POWER OF YOUR MIND, SELF-SABOTAGE AND SELF-COACHING	15
CHAPTER ONE - THE HIDDEN FORCES SHAPING YOUR MIND	17
What This Chapter Covers:	18
1.01 The Key to Professional Success	18
1.02 The Two Thinking Systems	20
1.03 The Mind Quiz	21
1.04 Mind Quiz Insights: Part 1	22
1.05 Mind Quiz Insights: Part 2	23
Chapter Summary	26
What's Next?	26
CHAPTER TWO - HOW SELF-SABOTAGE UNDERMINES SUCCESS (AND HOW TO STOP IT)	27
What This Chapter Covers:	28
2.01 The Origins of System 1's Programming	28
2.02 The Success Cycle	31
2.03 The Power of Self-Coaching	36
2.04 The Science of Change	38
2.05 Recognising the Impact of Self-Sabotage	40
2.06 Making Change Stick	42
Chapter Summary	44
What's Next?	45
PART TWO - MASTERING THE CORE SKILLS FOR UNSTOPPABLE CONFIDENCE, COURAGE AND RESILIENCE	47
CHAPTER THREE - THE SCIENCE OF OUTER CONFIDENCE: UNLOCKING YOUR PRESENCE	49
What This Chapter Covers:	51
3.01 Assessing Your Confidence	51
3.02 First Impressions	55
3.03 Why You Judge People	56
3.04 How Your Mind Filters The World	57
3.05 How Your Mind Deletes The World	59
3.06 How Your Mind Generalises The World	61
3.07 How Your Mind Distorts The World	62
3.08 How First Impressions Shape Success	63
3.09 What First Impression Do You make?	67

Chapter Summary	69
What's Next?	70

CHAPTER FOUR - BUILDING OUTER CONFIDENCE: ESSENTIAL SKILLS FOR PRESENCE AND IMPACT — 71

What This Chapter Covers:	72
4.01 Appearance	73
4.02 Posture	75
4.03 Smile	76
4.04 Eye contact	77
4.05 Gestures	78
4.06 Pace	80
4.07 Pitch	81
4.08 Filler Words	82
Chapter Summary	84
What's Next?	84

CHAPTER FIVE - THE SCIENCE OF ASSERTIVENESS: FINDING YOUR VOICE — 87

What This Chapter Covers:	89
5.01 Assessing Your Assertiveness	89
5.02 Understanding the Spectrum of Workplace Behaviours	91
5.03 How Behaviour Choices Shape Workplace Dynamics	94
5.04 Why Do People React Non-Assertively?	98
5.05 Non-Assertive Behaviour in Action	99
5.06 What Stops People Being Assertive?	101
5.07 Is Assertiveness Always the Best Option?	103
5.08 Who Are You Non-Assertive With?	104
Chapter Summary	107
What's Next?	107

CHAPTER SIX - BUILDING ASSERTIVENESS: THE SKILLS YOU NEED — 109

What This Chapter Covers:	110
6.01 Top Tips for Being More Assertive NOW	110
6.02 A Step-by-Step Approach to Being Assertive	112
6.03 How to Have an Assertive Conversation	117
6.04 Sam Confronts Belle and Muhammed	119
6.05 How to Decide in the Heat of the Moment	123
Chapter Summary	127
What's Next?	127

CHAPTER SEVEN - THE PSYCHOLOGY OF COURAGE: WHY WE HESITATE — 129

What This Chapter Covers:	130
7.01 Assessing Your Courage	131
7.02 Emotions Versus Feelings	133
7.03 What Determines How You Feel?	137

7.04 What Lies at the Core of Courage?	138
7.05 How Meanings Shape Your Reality	141
Chapter Summary	147
What's Next?	147

CHAPTER EIGHT - CULTIVATING COURAGE: THE SKILLS TO FACE FEAR HEAD-ON — 149

What This Chapter Covers:	150
8.01 Quick Fixes To Feel More Courageous	151
8.02 A Technique for Feeling Courageous	155
8.03 A Step-By-Step Process	159
8.04 Reframing: Practice with General Examples	161
8.05 Reframing: Practice with Your Own Objectives	163
Chapter Summary	166
What's Next?	166

CHAPTER NINE - THE SCIENCE OF RESILIENCE: BOUNCING BACK STRONGER — 167

What This Chapter Covers:	169
9.01 Assessing Your Resilience	169
9.02 Everyday Signs of Struggling with Resilience	171
9.03 Common Self-Talk Themes	174
9.04 Why Does Negative Thinking Dominate?	175
9.05 How Your Thoughts Are Generalised	178
9.06 How Your Thoughts Are Deleted	180
9.07 How Your Thoughts Are Distorted	182
Chapter Summary	188
What's Next?	188

CHAPTER TEN - BUILDING RESILIENCE: KEY SKILLS FOR ENDURANCE AND GROWTH — 189

What This Chapter Covers:	190
10.01 Silencing Your Inner Critic	190
10.02 Challenging Generalisations	193
10.03 Challenging Deletions	196
10.04 Challenging Distortions	198
Chapter Summary	211
What's Next?	212

PART THREE - REPROGRAMMING YOUR MIND FOR UNSHAKEABLE SELF-BELIEF — 215

CHAPTER ELEVEN - THE INNER MECHANICS OF LASTING CONFIDENCE — 217

What This Chapter Covers:	219
11.01 Hidden Programming	219
11.02 How Programmes Shape Reality	220

11.03 Reality Quiz	223
11.04 Unveiling Reality: Answers to the Reality Quiz	225
11.05 What the Quiz Reveals About Your Reality	227
11.06 When Programmes Fail You	229
11.07 What the Programmes Are	235
11.08 How Change Is Possible	236
Chapter Summary	237
What's Next?	238

CHAPTER TWELVE - CHANGE YOUR CORE CONFIDENCE — PERMANENTLY — 239

What This Chapter Covers:	241
12.01 Identifying Limiting Beliefs	241
12.02 Networks of Beliefs	243
12.03 The Root Cause of Beliefs	244
12.04 The Marvel of Identifying Limiting Beliefs	246
12.05 Seeking Contrary Evidence	247
12.06 Challenging Mental Filters	248
12.07 Practicing Challenging Limiting Belief Filters	250
12.08 Challenging Your Limiting Beliefs	254
12.09 Rewiring Your Brain	256
12.10 Short-Cut to Success	260
Chapter Summary	265
What's Next?	265

ABOUT THE AUTHOR	269
ACKNOWLEDGEMENTS	271
BIBLIOGRAPHY	273

ABOUT THE BOOK

Welcome to The Confidence Breakthrough—a practical guide to overcoming self-doubt and building lasting confidence, courage, and resilience.

Based on over 30 years of research and experience, this book blends neuroscience, psychology, and proven self-coaching methods. Through relatable examples and interactive exercises, you'll learn how to rewire self-limiting patterns and unlock your potential to lead and succeed.

This isn't just about feeling confident—it's about creating a breakthrough in how you think, feel, act, and grow. You'll gain the tools to overcome inner blocks, tackle challenges, and create meaningful, long-term change.

The book stands alone or works alongside the online course of the same name, which includes guided lessons, interactive activities, and avatar-led role-plays. If you're enrolled in the course, this book deepens and reinforces your learning. If not, you'll still find practical strategies here that you can apply immediately.

The Confidence Breakthrough is structured into three parts and twelve chapters, each filled with actionable tools to help you break through limits and build sustainable confidence.

PART ONE: UNDERSTANDING THE POWER OF YOUR MIND, SELF-SABOTAGE AND SELF-COACHING

Explore the hidden forces that shape your thoughts, emotions, and actions, either propelling you forward or holding you back. Using insights from neuroscience, you'll learn how to reprogramme unhelpful patterns and harness the power of your mind. Self-coaching is introduced as a key tool for taking control of your growth.

PART TWO: MASTERING THE CORE SKILLS FOR UNSTOPPABLE CONFIDENCE, COURAGE AND RESILIENCE

Confidence, assertiveness, courage, and resilience are essential for professional success. This section reveals the science behind these traits, the unconscious patterns that influence them, and how to use self-coaching to strengthen each one, empowering you to act boldly and thrive.

PART THREE: REPROGRAMMING YOUR MIND FOR UNSHAKEABLE SELF-BELIEF

Even high achievers face self-doubt and limiting behaviours. This section explains why we sabotage ourselves and how to replace fear with confidence. You'll learn how to rewire your thinking, build lasting self-trust, and create a mindset of empowerment and long-term success.

> *Disclaimer: This book is for informational and motivational purposes only. It is not a substitute for professional, therapeutic, medical, or mental health advice.*

MEET SAM

Throughout the book, you will follow the journey of Sam, a fictional character who I've written to reflect the complexities of real-world workplace challenges. Her experiences are designed to resonate with you, offering insights and lessons that complement your own growth.

Let's meet Sam now:

Sam is a twenty-five-year-old, highly capable, organised, and resourceful Project Coordinator who has been performing her job effectively since leaving university. Her abilities were reflected in her recent promotion to a Team Leader position. While she is generally well-regarded by her colleagues and gets along well with her team, Sam finds it difficult to manage one particular individual who is twice her age.

Although Sam loves her job and the organisation for which she works, she feels frustrated that she's not progressing as fast as she would like. However, she appreciates that her promotion to Team Leader is a step in the right direction. While her goal is to be a Project Manager, she doesn't have time to be proactive or gain additional experience because she's too busy being reactive as she battles her endless to-do list. This leads to sleepless nights, not least because she often gets up in the middle of the night to work just to keep on top of it all. Inevitably, she wakes up feeling exhausted and stressed.

Sam has made it clear to her manager that she wants to be promoted to Project Manager. While her manager agrees that Sam is more than capable skill-wise, she has suggested that Sam needs to improve certain soft skills. These include speaking up more in meetings, being more authoritative (especially with her team and new clients), being more confident in herself and her abilities, and managing her workload more effectively.

As painful as it is to hear, Sam knows her manager is right: she struggles to say 'I can do this' and even downplays her capabilities. She also finds it difficult to set boundaries, which means she always has more work than she can handle. This leads her to feel resentment towards her colleagues, who seem to have minimal work while she struggles to keep on top of her ever-growing to-do list.

The situation is further complicated by her colleague, who doesn't do what she asks. When Sam tries to assert herself with him, she struggles to find the right words, feels embarrassed, and ends up doing the work herself. This only adds to her already overwhelming to-do list.

In meetings, Sam wants to speak up and often has good ideas, but she keeps quiet. Then, frustratingly, someone else says what she was thinking and gets praised for it.

Sam feels frustrated that she knows what she needs to change, but doesn't know how to.

Is there any part of Sam's description that you recognise in yourself? If so, it's not surprising. I've met thousands of 'Sams' (both male and female) over my many years of coaching and training—people who have more than enough capability, skill, and experience to advance in their careers but are held back by a hard-to-pinpoint 'something'. Alternatively, they are so crippled by stress, worry, and the pressure of an endless workload that they can't think beyond just getting through each day.

If you sense something is holding you back from advancing in your career, it's possible that your own mind is creating barriers to your success and your being able to fulfil your potential at work—without you even realising it. If that resonates with you, this book is here to help!

PART ONE

UNDERSTANDING THE POWER OF YOUR MIND, SELF-SABOTAGE AND SELF-COACHING

Part One comprises two chapters in which you will discover how your mind operates and learn the hidden forces that shape your thoughts, feelings, and actions. These forces can either work in your favour—driving success—or hold you back through self-sabotage and frustration. You'll gain insight into why certain behaviours—no matter how illogical they seem—can hold you back from the confidence and success you deserve.

The power of your mind is incredible, and neuroscience-backed insights will help you learn how it is possible to reprogramme unhelpful mental patterns and harness the full power of your mind for success. Additionally, you'll be introduced to self-coaching—a transformative technique that enables you to take control of your own development, helping you break through mental barriers and unlock your full potential.

1

THE HIDDEN FORCES SHAPING YOUR MIND

> *"You have power over your mind – not outside events. Realise this, and you will find strength."*
> **Marcus Aurelius**[1]

Every day, Sam encounters situations that leave her feeling frustrated, annoyed, or stressed. Because these external events and her emotional responses occur simultaneously, she assumes that the events themselves are responsible for her feelings. This allows her to place blame on something or someone outside of herself.

For example, when her colleague, Muhammed, fails to complete a task she assigned to him, she feels a surge of anger and attributes her stress to his inaction. Or when Belle, her manager, asks her to take on a new task while she's already feeling overwhelmed, she grows frustrated and blames her colleagues for not pulling their weight.

Do you ever feel like Sam? Do situations at work seem beyond your control, making you feel triumphant one moment and stressed the next? If so, you're not alone. As a human being with a brain, your

---

[1] *Marcus Aurelius was Roman emperor from 161 to 180 AD and a Stoic philosopher.*

mind is constantly guiding your thoughts and emotions—shaping your experience of reality, often without you even realising it. Most of the time, this works in your favour. At times, though, it can also lead to self-sabotage, pushing you further from what you truly want.

The problem is that you weren't born with an instruction manual for your brain. As a result, it largely operates on autopilot—without conscious effort or input from you. If the idea that your mind controls your thoughts, feelings, and actions—even in ways you don't always intend—feels unsettling, there's good news: while your mind can create obstacles in your professional life, it also holds the key to overcoming them. That's why understanding how your mind works is essential.

Once you recognise the consequences of leaving your mind on autopilot, you can begin using self-coaching to unlock your full potential—becoming more confident, courageous, and resilient in your career.

What This Chapter Covers:

- 1.01 The Key to Professional Success
- 1.02 The Two Thinking Systems
- 1.03 The Mind Quiz
- 1.04 Mind Quiz Insights: Part 1
- 1.05 Mind Quiz Insights: Part 2

1.01 The Key to Professional Success

Your brain is an extraordinary powerhouse. Did you know it can send up to 100,000 trillion messages per second while using no more energy than a refrigerator light bulb? In contrast, a supercomputer capable of processing the same volume of information would require an entire hydroelectric power plant.[2]

---

[2] Lewis, J. and Webster, A. (2014) Sort Your Brain Out. Capstone.

But beyond its raw capacity, what's truly remarkable is how your brain works. It doesn't just process information: it actively shapes your experience of the world. It influences how you approach challenges, manage stress, and, ultimately, how confident you feel in your decisions.

Every day, your brain makes around 35,000 decisions—from simple choices (like whether to have a salad or a sandwich) to complex ones (such as switching careers or staying put). What's fascinating is that most of these decisions happen outside of your conscious awareness. Even when you feel like you're making a rational choice, much of your reasoning occurs beneath the surface.

This is why it's crucial to understand how your mind operates—because your thoughts directly impact your confidence, assertiveness, and resilience.

How Your Mind Shapes Your Actions

Imagine this scenario:

Your manager offers you a high-profile project, a fantastic opportunity for career growth. But when the moment comes to respond, you hesitate. Even though you have the skills, you remain silent—not because you don't want the opportunity, but because you don't want to "rock the boat."

On the surface, it seems like you didn't make a decision at all. In reality, however, you did—you chose to stay quiet.

Now picture this:

You're overwhelmed with deadlines, yet when a colleague asks for your help with an urgent task, you say yes—despite already being stretched thin. Again, it might feel like you had no choice. In reality, though, you chose to take on more work instead of setting boundaries.

These responses may feel automatic, but they stem from hidden forces within your mind. To understand why you act the way you do, you need to explore the two distinct systems that drive your thinking.

1.02 The Two Thinking Systems

While your brain isn't physically divided into two parts, thinking about it in this way helps to understand how it functions. In his bestselling book, *Thinking, Fast and Slow*, Daniel Kahneman describes two distinct systems that govern our decision-making:

- **System 1:** Fast, automatic, intuitive, and emotional. It requires little effort and operates in the background, helping you handle routine tasks effortlessly.

- **System 2:** Slow, logical, analytical, and effortful. It steps in when you need to make decisions, solve problems, or think critically.

Most of the time, these systems work together seamlessly.

"Systems 1 and 2 are both active whenever we are awake. System 1 runs automatically, while System 2 operates in a comfortable, low-effort mode. System 1 continuously generates suggestions for System 2: impressions, intuitions, intentions, and feelings. If endorsed by System 2, these impressions become beliefs, and impulses become voluntary actions. When all goes smoothly, System 2 accepts System 1's suggestions with little or no modification." — Daniel Kahneman

In other words, System 1 effortlessly handles routine decisions, allowing you to perform everyday tasks with little or no conscious effort—such as driving safely from A to B. However, when an unexpected challenge arises, perhaps there's an unexpected road closure, System 2 activates, analysing the situation and determining the best course of action.

Efficiency: Why System 1 Dominates

Your brain prefers System 1 because it's efficient. From an evolutionary perspective, conserving mental energy was critical for survival—our ancestors couldn't afford to overthink every decision.

As a result, System 1 evolved to handle most decisions on autopilot, which Kahneman refers to as *cognitive ease;* System 2 then kicks in only when necessary. This shift to more effortful thinking causes *cognitive strain.*

- **COGNITIVE EASE:** System 1 relies on habits and past experiences to keep life running smoothly. It's why you instinctively grab your usual coffee mug or follow the same route to work without thinking.
- **COGNITIVE STRAIN:** When System 2 is engaged, thinking requires more effort. Solving a maths problem, making a tough decision, or analysing complex data demands System 2's deeper processing.

To experience the interplay between System 1 and System 2, complete this Mind Quiz.

1.03 The Mind Quiz

Answer the following six questions quickly (within a maximum of five seconds each). Don't try to over-think or second-guess yourself: go with your first instinct.

1. How many legs does a dog have?
2. What colour is the sky on a clear day?
3. What sound does a cat make?
4. How many seconds are in 56 days?
5. You're considering two investment options:
    - Option 1: There's a 15% chance you'll lose all your money.
    - Option 2: There's an 85% chance you'll keep all your money.

    Which do you choose?

6. A lake has a patch of lily pads that doubles in size every day. If it takes 48 days for the patch to cover the entire lake, how many days does it take for it to cover half the lake?

Let's find out how you did and explore which thinking system you used while answering each question.

1.04 Mind Quiz Insights: Part 1

We'll start by looking at the first four questions.

Question 1 (How many legs does a dog have?): You likely answered '4' quickly, without much thought, because this is an easy, instinctual answer that your brain automatically knows. This is System 1 thinking at work.

Question 2 (What colour is the sky on a clear day?): You again probably answered 'Blue' instantly because System 1 thinking quickly retrieved this information without effort.

Question 3 (What sound does a cat make?): Again, you likely thought 'meow' as it's an easy, automatic response based on experience. This is another great example of System 1's ability to give rapid answers based on experience.

The fact that you knew all these answers without hesitation demonstrates the incredible power of System 1. Here, you experienced cognitive ease in action—fast, effortless, and automatic. System 1, with its vast library of stored knowledge and instinctual reasoning, provided accurate answers in all three cases. It's a testament to how efficiently this system supports you in navigating daily life, even as you juggle multiple demands at work.

Question 4 (How many seconds are there in 56 days?): The correct answer is 4,838,400 seconds—but unless you're a math whiz, you probably didn't get it in five seconds. That's because System 1 recognised its limit and handed the problem to System 2. Since System 2 requires effort and time, you likely didn't have enough time to process the answer.

These four questions were designed to highlight the seamless transition between the two thinking systems. System 1 knows its limitations, and when it encounters a problem beyond its expertise, it delegates to System 2. If you had more time, engaging System 2 might have helped you solve the problem, but you would have felt the mental strain—this is *cognitive strain*.

Question 4 highlights an important truth about *cognitive strain*: while System 2 is powerful, it's energy-intensive and can only be sustained for short periods. This mirrors workplace challenges that require deep thinking, analysis, and decision-making. While System 1 keeps you running smoothly most of the time, System 2 is your problem-solving powerhouse—but overuse can lead to mental fatigue.

The Harmony of Two Systems

The first four questions illustrate the brilliance of Kahneman's insight: "When all goes smoothly, which is most of the time, System 2 adopts the suggestions of System 1 with little or no modification."

Together, the two systems enable you to operate efficiently on autopilot while maintaining the capacity for deep thinking when required. However, not every decision unfolds seamlessly, as the exploration of questions 5 and 6 will reveal.

1.05 Mind Quiz Insights: Part 2

Let's now explore your answers to question 5 and 6.

> **Question 5 (Investment Opportunity):** Did you choose Option 2? If so, you're in the majority: most people would instinctively opt for a 85% chance of keeping all their money, as opposed to a 15% chance of losing everything – despite both options actually offering the same odds.
>
> Why do most people choose option 2? It's because this option instinctively sounds the most appealing: System 1 reacts quickly and

favours the positive framing, rather than taking the time to evaluate the actual probability. This tendency is known as framing bias, where the way information is presented influences decision-making.

This question illustrates how System 1 can confidently provide its best guess, and System 2, preferring cognitive ease over cognitive strain, accepts it without question. In this case, System 1's response wasn't problematic, as both options were mathematically identical. However, this blind trust in System 1's conclusions can be easily manipulated.

How This Behaviour Affects Everyday Decisions

Retailers frequently exploit System 1's preference for cognitive ease—and instant gratification—to influence the purchasing decisions made by customers.

For example, imagine you return a jumper after realising you bought it on impulse. Feeling proud for saving the £20 you originally spent, you spot a "Today Only" sale sign for a pair of trainers:

"Was £120, now only £75!"

Immediately, System 1 registers this as a great bargain, urging you to act before the price goes back up. However, if you paused to engage System 2, you might compare prices elsewhere and discover that £75 is actually the regular price: the original £120 was artificially inflated to create the illusion of a discount.

Even worse, since the trainers are marked as a sale item, the store's "no returns" policy prevents you from changing your mind later—a classic case of buyer's remorse.

This technique works by anchoring your perception of value to an inflated reference point, making the offer seem better than it is. By pausing and activating System 2, you can see through the manipulation and make a more informed decision. You might even realise you don't actually need another pair of trainers or that you could find a better deal elsewhere.

Without engaging System 2, however, you might spend money you don't have, derailing long-term financial goals such as paying off credit card debt. This subtle act of self-sabotage stems from System 1's unchecked dominance.

> **Question 6 (Lily Pads):** Did you confidently conclude that the lake would be covered in 24 days? If so, you're not alone. Halving 48 seems intuitive and requires minimal effort, making it an appealing answer. However, it's incorrect.

The correct answer is 47 days. Engaging System 2 reveals why: since the lily pads double in size each day, the lake would be half-covered on day 47, just one day before being fully covered.

This question was designed to expose a flaw in the dual-system approach. System 1 confidently offered its best guess, and because the answer felt right, System 2 didn't bother verifying it. Unlike Question 5, where the stakes were low, here the wrong answer has significant implications. System 2's failure to engage led to an error.

The key takeaway is that System 1 can be so confident in its answer that it doesn't recognise the need for System 2's help. This is where the danger lies—because when you fully trust your initial instinct, you do not realise you're making an error, just as you might be blind to how you're self-sabotaging at work.

The Workplace Implications

At work, this same System 1 / System 2 dynamic can lead to misjudgements, as quick answers that feel right may actually be flawed.

Imagine a team project misses its deadline. System 1 might immediately conclude:

> *"The problem is Darian—he's always slow to deliver."*

Since this explanation seems obvious and aligns with past experiences, System 2 doesn't step in to question it.

However, if you paused to analyse the situation, you might uncover the real cause: unclear timelines, poor communication, or a lack of resources affecting the entire team. Just like we saw with the lily pad problem, System 1 provided a quick but incorrect answer; because it felt intuitively correct, System 2 didn't intervene. As a result, the root issue remains unaddressed, and unfair blame is placed on an individual instead of the actual problem being fixed.

This example highlights how System 1's overconfidence in its first conclusion can lead to:

- Poor decision-making
- Unnecessary conflict
- Missed opportunities for improvement

Unfortunately, you can't simply force System 2 to engage—System 1's natural dominance is such that you won't be aware that System 1 has made an error. This is why a different approach is needed—and we explore this approach in Part 3.

Chapter Summary

By recognising the dual nature of your mind, you can better understand its preference for cognitive ease, which often allows System 1 to operate on autopilot. While this default mode is generally efficient—enabling System 1 and System 2 to work together seamlessly—there are times when they fall out of sync, leading to self-sabotage. Instead of helping you achieve your goals, your mind may inadvertently hold you back.

What's Next?

If a lack of confidence, courage, or resilience is preventing you from achieving your professional goals, it's a sign that System 1 and System 2 are misaligned. Your mission is to restore harmony between them.

How? That's exactly what you'll discover in the next chapter.

2

HOW SELF-SABOTAGE UNDERMINES SUCCESS (AND HOW TO STOP IT)

"Self-doubt does more to sabotage individual potential than all external limitations put together."[3]
Brian Tracy

In the short to medium term, Sam has a clear vision of professional success: becoming a Project Manager at her current organisation. She loves what she does, knows what she wants, and is both motivated and hardworking—yet she still isn't achieving her goal. Understandably, this frustrates her, and she feels stuck, unsure of how to move forward. As she sees it, the quickest fix would be to apply for Project Management roles elsewhere. After all, a new job wouldn't just bring fresh opportunities—it would also mean no longer having to deal with Muhammed's defiance!

If, like Sam, you are wondering how to move forward, you need to learn another secret before you do anything potentially rash like quitting your job and looking for a new one elsewhere. (This secret is in addition to the fact that your problems exist inside of you not

---

[3] Brian Tracy. Canadian-American motivational public speaker and self-development author.

outside of you, and are due to the misalignment of the two thinking systems.) This second secret is that success is not an accident and has nothing to do with luck or circumstance. Rather, it has everything to do with—you've guessed it—your mind.

This chapter shares a formula to show you that success is created by thinking, feeling and behaving in a specific way, which means it is possible for *anyone* to be successful. It can help you understand more about how your inner world—your mind—determines the results you get in the outer world.

So, before you look for a new job in an attempt to solve your current problems, read this chapter first. Otherwise, you might find yourself encountering the same problems at your new place of work before long, just with different people, and in different situations.

What This Chapter Covers:

- 2.01 The Origins of System 1's Programming
- 2.02 The Success Cycle
- 2.03 The Power of Self-Coaching
- 2.04 The Science of Change
- 2.05 Recognising the Impact of Self-Sabotage
- 2.06 Making Change Stick

2.01 The Origins of System 1's Programming

In Chapter 1, you learned about your mind's predominant reliance on System 1. The next question is: How does it make the decisions it makes? To answer this, we need to explore how System 1 is programmed.

Much like a highly advanced computer, your brain operates using a set of instructions—rules and guidelines that help it function efficiently. However, these rules are not consciously chosen. Instead, they are ingrained from a young age, shaped by societal norms, family expectations, and cultural values.

For example, if you are raised in Japan, one societal norm is that you should be quiet in public spaces, such as trains, because it's considered a sign of respect. By contrast, in Brazil, engaging in lively conversations on a train, or in similar public spaces—even with strangers—is seen as a sign of respect. Similarly, in some cultures, being exactly on time for a meeting is seen as a mark of professionalism; in others, arriving a few minutes late is considered normal, or even polite.

These differences highlight an important truth: There is no universal 'right' or 'wrong' set of rules—only those designed to help you navigate your specific environment.

By understanding the origins of these rules, you gain greater insight into how System 1 develops and influences your behaviour. While these ingrained responses may sometimes support your goals, other times, they may hold you back.

Why We Absorb Social Rules

Why do humans adopt social rules so readily? The answer lies in our evolutionary past.

In a dangerous and unpredictable world, survival depended on cooperation and group belonging. Being part of a group meant access to safety, food, and support, while exclusion could be life-threatening. This deep-rooted need to fit in and belong is a survival mechanism that continues to shape our thoughts and actions today.

From birth, you begin absorbing rules that help you navigate social, cultural, and familial environments. These early lessons form the foundations of your thoughts, feelings, and behaviours—often without you even realising it.

How System 1 Becomes Programmed

When you first learn something new—whether it's walking, reading, or driving—you engage System 2, the slower, more effortful part of your brain. Initially, these tasks are mentally exhausting: you have to concentrate hard and make deliberate choices at every step. But over time, your brain seeks efficiency.

The basal ganglia—the part of the brain responsible for habit formation—steps in and says, "We can't keep expending this much energy on repetitive tasks." So, it automates the behaviour, shifting it from System 2 to System 1. At this point, the action becomes effortless and instinctual.

This is why, after enough practice, activities like typing, driving, or even responding to social cues feel second nature: you no longer have to think about them consciously.

To illustrate this point, imagine your mind as an iceberg:

- The small tip above the water represents System 2—your conscious awareness and deliberate thought.
- The vast, hidden mass below the water line represents System 1—a storehouse of unconscious habits, learned skills, and deeply ingrained rules that are running on autopilot.

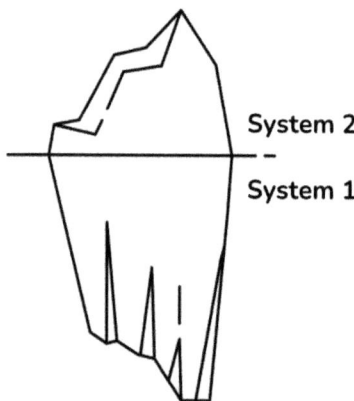

Everything you've mastered through repetition—whether it's tying your shoelaces or following societal norms—resides in System 1. It operates quietly in the background, shaping your thoughts, feelings, behaviours, and decisions.

The Hidden Influence of Early Programming

The same process of learned behaviours becoming embedded in System 1 also applies to the rules you absorbed as a child—both the broad societal norms you encountered and the specific expectations instilled by your family.

At first, these rules required effort and conscious attention, meaning they engaged System 2. But as you repeatedly followed them, they transitioned into System 1's database of stored instructions. Over time, they became ingrained as 'programmes' that automatically guide your behaviour without requiring conscious thought.

Now that you understand how System 1 becomes programmed, you'll soon discover how your confidence, courage, and resilience are directly shaped by the patterns and programmes embedded in System 1—and how they either create success or failure for you at work. Let's look at the Success Cycle to find out how.

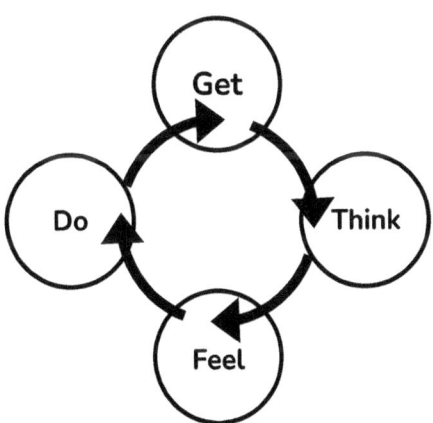

2.02 The Success Cycle

While you may not always realise it, many of the unconscious 'programmes' running in System 1 shape your thoughts, feelings, and behaviours, and ultimately determine your levels of confidence, courage, and resilience. Consider how these elements interact:

- Your thoughts influence your resilience—if you believe you can't handle a challenge, you may avoid taking action altogether.

- Your feelings affect your courage—if fear dominates your emotions, you might hesitate to take a necessary risk.

- Your behaviour impacts your confidence—if you act in an uncertain or hesitant way, you reinforce self-doubt and diminish your ability to assert yourself.

To understand why this happens, let's explore a concept called the Success Cycle, which explains how your internal processes create your external reality. This cycle operates as follows:

1. Your thoughts influence how you feel.
2. Your feelings affect what you do.
3. Your actions determine your results.
4. Your results reinforce your thoughts, continuing the cycle.

This cycle can either flow in a positive or negative direction, depending on whether your thoughts, feelings, and behaviours create what you would consider positive or negative results.

Let's consider an example. Imagine you are about to give a presentation at work. If you think *'I know my material well, and I'm going to deliver this confidently'*, you'll likely feel calm and self-assured. This mindset allows you to present clearly and engage your audience. As a result, the presentation goes well, reinforcing your thoughts of being capable.

Now, let's flip the scenario. Suppose you think *'I'm terrible at public speaking—everyone will see how nervous I am'*. This thought triggers feelings of anxiety, making your hands shake and your voice waver. You might rush through your slides, struggling to connect with the audience. If the presentation doesn't go well, it confirms your original thoughts, making you even more anxious the next time you have to speak in public.

The following is an activity to help you analyse your Success Cycle. You can read Sam's answers after each activity for clarity.

Activity 1a: Success

Think of a situation in which you achieved success at work—for example, an interview, a sales call, a promotion, or even confidently saying 'no' to your boss. Reflect on the following questions:

- What was the situation?
- What were your thoughts?
- What were your feelings?
- What were your actions?
- What was the result?

Activity 1a – Sam's Answer:

"My manager asked me to deliver a presentation to ten important stakeholders. I felt proud that she trusted me with such a crucial task, and since she gave me plenty of notice, I had ample time to prepare. I practised until I knew the material inside out and anticipated possible questions, researching answers to ensure I was ready for anything. I rehearsed repeatedly until I felt fully confident.

Naturally, I was nervous when I stood up to present, but I reminded myself that I was well-prepared. I covered all the material and finished precisely within the timeframe I had rehearsed. My manager, Belle, provided excellent feedback afterward. In her words, 'You nailed it!' As a result, she wouldn't hesitate to assign me another high-profile presentation, which aligns with my goal of securing a promotion."

Activity 1b: Failure

Now, think of a time when you experienced a setback at work—perhaps an unsuccessful interview, a missed promotion, or a situation in which you regretted not asserting yourself. Answer the same questions:

- What was the situation?
- What were your thoughts?
- What were your feelings?
- What were your actions?
- What was the result?

Activity 1b – Sam's Answer:

"Another manager asked me to work on a project with him. I was already overwhelmed with work, but I felt unable to say 'no.' Instead, I smiled and agreed, even though I was seething inside. Throughout the project, I kept thinking, 'I should have said no!' This led to feelings of resentment, especially when I found myself working on it late into the night.

Because I was disengaged, I only did the bare minimum. Unsurprisingly, the feedback I received was merely 'satisfactory.' As a result, I doubt that manager will ask me to collaborate again. While this may seem like a relief, it could also harm my chances of promotion in the long run."

Activity 1c: Differences

Compare your answers from Activities 1a and 1b. What differences do you notice in your thoughts, feelings, and results?

Activity 1c – Sam's Answer:

"The biggest difference was my level of motivation. In the success scenario, I felt excited because I wanted to do the task, had the time to prepare, and knew it would benefit my career. In contrast, in the failure scenario, I felt resentment—partly because I didn't have the time or capacity but also because I didn't see how it would help me.

It's no surprise that I received positive feedback in the scenario in which I felt motivated and engaged, and negative feedback when I felt resentful. Now that I reflect on it, had I done a good job, that manager's positive feedback could have contributed to my promotion. Maybe I need to rethink my approach!"

Are you surprised by what you've discovered? This exercise provides your first glimpse into how the Success Cycle creates positive or negative outcomes based on your thoughts, emotions, and behaviours. Before we move on, however, it's important to note that the Success Cycle isn't always a straightforward, linear process. There are nuances.

Nuances of The Success Cycle

At first glance, the Success Cycle may seem to flow in a single direction. However, different elements can influence one another in a more fluid way. For instance:

- Behaviour can change thoughts and feelings. Even if you don't feel confident, acting confidently—standing tall, speaking with conviction, and making eye contact—can trick your brain into thinking you are self-assured, which in turn can strengthen how confident you feel.

- Resilience can develop through action. By persisting through setbacks and proving to yourself that you can handle challenges, you cultivate a stronger sense of courage and adaptability.

You might also find that an experience doesn't seem to fit neatly into the Success Cycle. But don't worry: real-life situations are often more complex. To illustrate this, let's look at how the Success Cycle might appear—at this stage—not to be true for Sam in the context of a job interview. Imagine that Sam ignores the advice at the beginning of this chapter and decides the quickest and easiest route to solve her problems and become Project Manager would be to move organisations. This is what happens:

> Sam applies for a Project Manager position at a competing firm. She thinks she won't get the job because the interview will be challenging, which makes her feel worried about it. That worry makes her do extensive research and practice interview questions with an HR friend to ensure she is fully prepared. This, in turn, enables her to appear (what she does) calm, knowledgeable and keen in the interview, and she gets offered the job.

Notice how Sam thought she wouldn't get the job but does. At first glance, this might seem like evidence that the Success Cycle doesn't work. However, once you learn what drives the Success Cycle in Part Three, you'll see why it actually does. (For context, although Sam was offered the position, she declined it: the thought of moving made her realise that, deep down, she wanted to stay because she loves where she works.)

For now, the key takeaway is that the cycle is always turning—regardless of direction—but the path to professional success lies in making it work for you. You can achieve this by harnessing the power of System 2, which is exactly what you'll learn in Part Two. But first, you need to understand self-coaching and how it can help you consciously influence the Success Cycle—turning challenges into opportunities and setbacks into stepping stones for growth.

2.03 The Power of Self-Coaching

The ability to navigate challenges, setbacks, and opportunities on your own is one of the most valuable skills you can develop in your career. This is where self-coaching comes in. Self-coaching is the practice of guiding yourself towards growth and transformation through three key steps:

1. **Focused self-reflection:** Bringing awareness to your thoughts, emotions, and behaviours.
2. **Strategic assessment:** Identifying unhelpful patterns of behaviour and evaluating their impact.

3. **Deliberate action:** Consciously shifting those patterns to create more empowering responses.

Self-coaching is about becoming attuned to the automatic thoughts, feelings, and behaviours driven by System 1. Remember, much of what you think, feel, and do stems from deep-seated 'programmes' that have been running in the background for years. Self-coaching helps you to recognise these 'programmes' and then use System 2—the logical, intentional part of your brain—to override, challenge, and replace them with new, empowering ones. With repetition, these new 'programmes' become embedded in System 1, causing a lasting shift in your thoughts, feelings and behaviour.

With consistent practice, self-coaching can take you from feeling like a passive victim of circumstances to becoming 'response-able'—capable of consciously choosing how you react to challenges. It empowers you to make bold, decisive choices, navigate obstacles with greater ease, and develop an unshakable belief in your ability to succeed. Ultimately, this process ensures that the Success Cycle works in your favour—reprogramming your mind to cultivate lasting confidence, courage, and resilience.

Bridging the Gap Between System 1 and System 2

In Question 5 of The Mind Quiz, you discovered that it's possible to override System 1's automatic reactions by engaging System 2. This is why, in Part Two of this book, you will learn how self-coaching can help you do exactly that. Essentially, you'll learn how to:

- Identify System 1's automatic thoughts, feelings, and behaviours that are causing you to self-sabotage and are directing your Success Cycle in a way that leads to the opposite of what you want.

- Use System 2 to override System 1's automatic thoughts, feelings, and behaviours, so you can become more confident, courageous, and resilient, driving your Success Cycle in the direction that brings you what you want.

Unfortunately, Part Two doesn't provide a solution to all your problems. As you learned in Question 6 of The Mind Quiz, there are times when System 1 is so confident in its answer that it doesn't recognise the need for help from System 2. Only by understanding your deep-rooted 'programmes'—what they *really* are—can you begin to appreciate that they need changing. For these situations, self-coaching offers a structured approach to using System 2 to rewire those 'programmes' by replacing them with new, empowering ones.

If you're wondering why we need to bother with Part Two—well, without it, Part Three won't make sense!

If you doubt that it's truly possible to change long-standing thoughts, feelings, and behaviours, next we will explore the science behind change to prove that it is indeed possible. You'll discover compelling evidence that transformation is not only achievable but well within your reach—regardless of your age or past experiences.

2.04 The Science of Change

Many people believe that once they reach adulthood, their brain is 'set' in its ways. If you've ever thought that it's too late to change how you think, break old habits, or develop new skills, think again. Your brain remains adaptable throughout your entire life, capable of forming new pathways and strengthening existing ones—and all thanks to a phenomenon called neuroplasticity.

For decades, scientists believed that the adult brain was like concrete—solidified and unchangeable after a certain age. However, research has revealed that the brain is more like clay—malleable, flexible, and capable of being reshaped at any stage of life. Neuroplasticity allows your brain to grow, learn, and evolve by forming new neural connections, proving that personal transformation is always within reach. Whether you want to boost your confidence, enhance resilience, or develop assertiveness, neuroplasticity ensures that you can rewire your brain to support those goals.

Neuroplasticity in Action

One of the most compelling examples of neuroplasticity can be seen in London's black cab drivers, who famously master *The Knowledge*—a mental map of 25,000 streets and 20,000 landmarks across the city. The process of memorising this vast network takes years of dedicated study, and brain scans show that, as cab drivers train, the hippocampus—the part of the brain responsible for memory—physically grows larger to accommodate the new neural connections required. Astonishingly, once they retire and stop using *The Knowledge* daily, their hippocampus returns to its original size.[4] This demonstrates that the brain continuously adapts to meet new demands and that learning is not a fixed process—it's a lifelong ability.

Neuroplasticity isn't just limited to taxi drivers or memory-based tasks. Consider someone who has always been shy and avoids public speaking. Initially, speaking in front of an audience triggers anxiety. With consistent practice, however, their brain rewires itself to handle the experience more comfortably. Over time, what once felt impossible becomes second nature. (This happened to me, and it helped me go from being petrified of public speaking to doing it for a living!)

Similarly, studies of stroke patients have shown how the brain can rewire itself to compensate for lost function. In some cases, individuals who lose the ability to use one hand after a stroke can retrain their brain to rely on the other hand, reinforcing new neural pathways through repetition. These examples highlight the brain's extraordinary capacity to adapt—whether to physical, emotional, or cognitive challenges.[5]

Why This Matters for You

The most exciting takeaway from neuroplasticity is this: your brain can change until the day you die. This is fantastic news: no matter

---

[4] Maguire, E. Gadian, D. Johnsrude, I and Frith,C. (2000) *Navigation-related structural change in the hippocampi of taxi drivers.* PNAS.

[5] Su, F and Xu, W. (2020) *Enhancing Brain Plasticity to Promote Stroke Recovery.* National Library of Medicine.

where you are in your professional journey, it is never too late to build confidence, courage, and resilience. If you've ever felt 'stuck' in patterns of self-doubt, self-sabotage or hesitation, remember that these patterns are not permanent. Just as you learned them, you can unlearn and replace them with more empowering habits.

By making deliberate efforts to reshape your thoughts, feelings, and behaviours, you can:

- Respond thoughtfully rather than react impulsively
- Step into your most confident and courageous self
- Build resilience to handle setbacks more effectively

This isn't about forcing yourself to change overnight. It's about small, consistent efforts that rewire your brain over time. Your mind is not static—it's a dynamic, ever-evolving masterpiece.

Before exploring how to take control of your professional success, take a moment to consider the consequences of *not* taking control of your mind and overcoming self-sabotage.

2.05 Recognising the Impact of Self-Sabotage

Let's think about a potential consequence of self-sabotage—namely, turning to external vices. These vices can manifest in various ways—food, caffeine, alcohol, social media, overworking, or even shopping.

 ### Activity 2: Identifying External Vices

Read the following six questions, and decide if any of them resonate with you.

1. Work Obsession

Are you obsessed with work? Do you work until you are physically exhausted? Do you rarely take holidays? Do you find it difficult to relax if you *do* take a break? Do your personal relationships and social life suffer as a result?

2. Caffeine Fix

Can you only function after you've had your first cuppa of the day? Do you rely on an energy drink to boost your energy and mood? Can you only come alive once you've had your caffeine quota? Do you get headaches and feel irritable if you abstain?

3. Food Junkie

Do you crave cakes, chocolate, sweets, and crisps? Do you stuff yourself until you feel physically sick? Do you feel guilty afterwards, and promise yourself to avoid these foods for the next month, only to fall off the wagon the very next day?

4. Social Media Fix

Do you check Facebook before you get out of bed in the morning? Do you tweet while you're watching TV? Do you scroll endlessly through TikTok when you should be working? Do you binge-watch YouTube videos? Do you feel anxious if you can't access Instagram? Do you panic if you're in a low signal area?

5. Drinking Habit

Do you go for a drink after work most nights? Do you always have an open bottle of wine 'on the go' in the fridge? Do you often have a drink to unwind or relax after work? Can you imagine being in a pub and not having a drink? Does the idea of being the 'designated driver' for a night out fill you with dread?

Activity 2 – Sam's Answer:

"I am a junk food addict. Often, I snack throughout the day because I'm too busy to eat a proper meal. But when I'm stressed or anxious, I take it to another level—I've been known to eat an entire tub of ice cream in one sitting. Of course, I feel annoyed with myself afterward, but before long, I do it again."

These vices are more common than you might think. While some vices seem harmless, they can lead to dependency over time. What starts as a coping mechanism can become a self-sabotaging habit.

According to the NHS, excessive caffeine can cause anxiety, restlessness, and irregular heartbeats. Over-consumption of junk food can lead to obesity, increasing the risk of serious health conditions. Social media addiction can trigger anxiety and depression due to reliance on dopamine-driven validation. Even work addiction can lead to burnout and strained personal relationships.

If you recognise an external vice in your life, the key is to acknowledge it. Ask yourself: *Could I stop if I wanted to?* If the answer is no, it may be time to take control of your mind.

2.06 Making Change Stick

As you move forward, your focus will be on engaging System 2, the part of your mind responsible for conscious decision-making, to ensure that your Success Cycle flows in a positive direction that achieves positive results for you at work. However, this will require sustained effort and energy. Change doesn't happen simply by wishing for it—it happens through intentional action.

To ensure you stay on track, it's essential to clarify what you want to get at work—in other words, what your objectives are. Let's think about this next.

Activity 3: Your Objectives

This activity is designed to help you clarify your System 2-driven objectives (your long-term, deliberate goals) and recognise how System 1's automatic reactions may lead to self-sabotaging behaviours. By bringing these patterns to light, you can begin to align your actions with your aspirations.

Step 1: Reflect on Your Aspirations

Think about the professional goals you could achieve if you had unshakeable confidence, courage and resilience. Use the prompts below to guide your reflection:

- What do you hope to achieve at work in the next 6 months or a year?
- What skills, habits, or outcomes do you want to develop through this book?
- Write down your answers as specific objectives to set a clear foundation for growth.

Step 2: Identify Self-Sabotaging Patterns

For each objective you've listed, reflect on behaviours, thoughts, or habits that may hinder your progress. Consider the following questions:

- What actions or inactions make it harder for you to achieve this goal?
- What automatic thoughts come to mind when you're working toward this objective?
- What habits or distractions pull you away from staying focused?

Document these patterns alongside your goals to uncover how System 1 influences your actions.

Step 3: Map the Conflict

Create a table to visually map the relationship between your objectives and self-sabotaging behaviours. Use the example on the next page. Keep your table handy and update it whenever you identify new goals or patterns during your learning journey. This exercise will serve as a roadmap to help you tackle challenges and make intentional progress toward your objectives. If this feels challenging, to help, Sam completes her table, offering ideas and insight into the objectives she'll focus on throughout the book.

Objective	Self-Sabotaging Behaviour
Complete a professional course	Procrastinate by overthinking assignments
Build confidence in public speaking	Avoid speaking opportunities out of fear
Delegate more of my work	Do it myself

Activity 3 - Sam's Answer:

Sam reflects on her goals and self-sabotaging patterns to create her table:

Objective	Self-Sabotaging Behaviour
Get Muhammed to do what I ask him to do	Avoid speaking to him about his behaviour
Speak up / Share my ideas in meetings	Keep quiet
Shout out about my strengths	Downplay my strengths
Speak to Belle about my colleagues doing more of their fair share of work	Avoid speaking to her / Do work myself i.e. don't delegate
Do new tasks outside of my comfort zone	Avoid doing any new tasks
Feel comfortable delivering last-minute presentations	Make excuses to avoid last-minute presentations
Be able to switch off from work	Work in the middle of the night
Be able to let go and move on when things don't go well	Focus on what I did wrong

By defining your goals now, you have a roadmap for transformation. This will give you clear focus areas and help you track the meaningful changes needed to build greater confidence, assertiveness, courage, and resilience at work.

Chapter Summary

System 1 is driven by 'programmes' that helped you survive and thrive in the society, culture, and family in which you were raised. The

Success Cycle shows how your thoughts, feelings, and actions create either positive or negative outcomes. When the cycle flows in a positive direction, leading to what you want, it's likely that System 1 and System 2 are working harmoniously together. Great! However, when the cycle leads to self-sabotage—and possibly reliance on an external vice—you may find yourself getting you the opposite of what you want. This is a clear sign that something's wrong. Understanding how the cycle works, and recognising its nuances in real-life situations, is key to navigating professional success.

Self-coaching can help you become aware of what lies behind the obstacles you face at work while enabling you to consciously engage System 2. This process allows you to take control over your automatic thoughts, feelings, and actions, leading to increased confidence, courage, and resilience. This will position you to redirect the Success Cycle to achieve your professional goals.

Self-coaching can also help to rewire the deep-rooted 'programmes' in System 1 with new, empowering ones. By taking these steps, you can focus on achieving your long-term objectives and build the foundation for greater success and fulfilment in your career.

What's Next?

Now that you have a solid understanding of how your mind works—particularly the two thinking systems and the Success Cycle, and how they can lead to self-sabotage when things don't go as planned—you're ready for the next step. In Part Two, you'll explore how to harness the power of System 2 to override System 1 when it's contributing to self-sabotage at work. You'll also uncover the science behind confidence, assertiveness, courage, and resilience, along with practical strategies to engage System 2 and boost success in each of these areas.

PART TWO:
MASTERING THE CORE SKILLS FOR UNSTOPPABLE CONFIDENCE, COURAGE AND RESILIENCE

In the second part of this book, we'll explore the four essential pillars of professional growth: confidence, assertiveness, courage, and resilience. There are eight chapters, with two chapters dedicated to each core trait.

In the first of each pair of chapters, we'll delve into the science behind each topic, uncovering how your brain processes these qualities and gaining a deeper understanding of why you behave the way you do—or don't—in certain situations. These insights will help you identify the hidden processes that may be holding you back, providing clarity on how to break free and move forward.

The second of each pair is focused on practical application. Here, you'll learn powerful self-coaching techniques tailored to each pillar of growth. You'll discover how to tap into the focused power of System 2 to override System 1's automatic reactions. You'll also develop actionable strategies and take meaningful steps to boost your confidence, strengthen your assertiveness, embrace courage, and build greater resilience.

By the end of Part Two, you'll have not only a solid understanding of how these traits function, but also the tools and techniques needed to transform the way you think, act, and respond—empowering you to thrive in your professional life.

THE SCIENCE OF OUTER CONFIDENCE: UNLOCKING YOUR PRESENCE

"What people say and feel about you when you've left a room is precisely your job while you are in it."
Rasheed Ogunlaru[6]

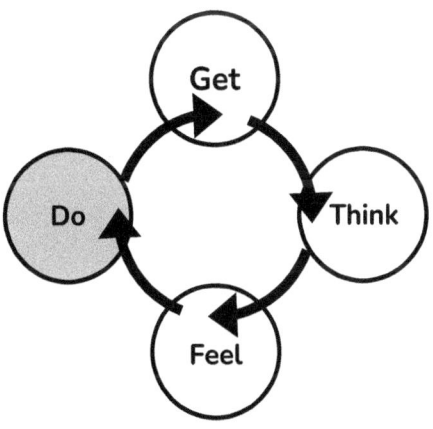

Sam has a meeting scheduled with a new internal client named Frank, whom she's never met before. She's feeling stressed, as her workload is already overwhelming, and she's

---

[6] Rasheed Ogunlaru is a leading life coach, motivational speaker and business coach partner to the British Library's Business and Intellectual Property Centre.

had another sleepless night. The last thing she needs is more work. When Sam enters the meeting, she's surprised to see Belle, her manager, already there, chatting animatedly with Frank. This immediately puts Sam on edge. She wasn't expecting Belle to join the meeting, and having her there makes Sam feel incapable.

Sam quietly enters the room, not wanting to disrupt their conversation, and avoids eye contact with either of them as she sits down next to Belle. When they finally stop talking, Belle introduces Sam to Frank, outlining her strengths as she does. Sam simply nods in acknowledgment but says nothing, feeling embarrassed by the compliments.

Frank then explains his needs but directs the conversation to Belle, never once looking at Sam. Sam focuses on taking notes, trying to appear engaged and attentive.

After the meeting, Belle informs Sam that Frank has requested Muhammed to take the lead on the project instead, as he thinks Sam is too junior and lacks the experience needed for such a high-profile task. Belle says she tried to persuade Frank to reconsider, but he's adamant that Sam didn't inspire confidence during the meeting.

While Sam feels a sense of relief at not being given more work, she's also upset that she failed to make a positive impression—especially given that she's the team leader. She had thought she was being humble, polite, and thoughtful. On top of that, she worries that this will make Muhammed even more difficult to manage, if that's possible.

In the example above, Sam gives Frank the impression that she's more junior and less experienced than she actually is. As a result, Frank lacks confidence in her ability to help him. This illustrates the power of first impressions.

While everyone makes an impression when they meet someone for the first time, do you know what kind of impression you make? Do you know whether, like Sam, you appear confident or not? And should you care? The answer is *yes*, because, as you will discover, first impressions matter a great deal. Throughout your professional life, you'll meet a series of new colleagues, clients, and stakeholders—people you'll interact with for anywhere from a few minutes to the entirety of your career.

In this chapter, we'll explore why first impressions matter, and why it is important to create the right impression consciously (what you do), so that the *Success Cycle* turns in the direction you want it to, and you can get what you want from your career. The next chapter then considers what you can do consciously to appear confident and create the right impression.

What This Chapter Covers:

- 3.01 Assessing Your Confidence
- 3.02 First Impressions
- 3.03 Why You Judge People
- 3.04 How Your Mind Filters The World
- 3.05 How Your Mind Deletes The World
- 3.06 How Your Mind Generalises The World
- 3.07 How Your Mind Distorts The World
- 3.08 How First Impressions Shape Success
- 3.09 What First Impression Do You make?

3.01 Assessing Your Confidence

Let's find out how confident you are—currently—in the workplace.

Activity 4: Assessing Your Confidence

Below are several scenarios that you may encounter in the workplace. After each scenario, you'll find two contrasting options. Take a moment to reflect on how you would respond, what you might feel, and how you would approach each situation. Then, select the option that most accurately reflects your typical reaction.

Scenario 1: After a period of working remotely, you are now asked to work more frequently in the office.

- **Option 1:** You feel excited at the prospect of engaging with colleagues face-to-face again, as you've found working remotely isolating.

- **Option 2:** You feel uneasy, as you've never met many of your colleagues in person and fear you might come across the wrong way or say something awkward.

Scenario 2: Your manager has invited you to attend a networking event next week.

- **Option 1:** You feel a little apprehensive but recognise the value of expanding your network, so you're willing to give it a try. After all, you never know who you might meet.

- **Option 2:** You feel overwhelmed and consider calling in sick, as you struggle with meeting strangers and find it difficult to sell yourself.

Scenario 3: You've been asked to deliver a presentation at the team meeting next week.

- **Option 1:** You feel comfortable, knowing that your audience consists of colleagues at a similar level, so the presentation should be straightforward.

- **Option 2:** You're anxious about making mistakes and worry you'll say something embarrassing.

Scenario 4: You've been invited to attend a senior leadership meeting next week. Would you contribute if you had something valuable to share?

- **Option 1:** Although nervous, you recognise the reason for your invitation and would speak up if you had something useful to add.
- **Option 2:** You feel intimidated, concerned that your lack of experience will be exposed, and worry you'll say something wrong.

Scenario 5: Your colleague, Rosie, tells you that a couple of team members mentioned they find you irritating because you tend to interrupt others.

- **Option 1:** You feel hurt but acknowledge the truth in what Rosie is saying. You appreciate her honesty and begin making a conscious effort to improve your communication.
- **Option 2:** You feel defensive and want to know who said it so you can avoid them, instead of addressing the issue constructively.

Scenario 6: You share your opinion in a team meeting, only to sense that a couple of colleagues didn't agree with you.

- **Option 1:** You take the opportunity to ask them for feedback, seeking to learn and improve through open discussion.
- Option 2: You dwell on it for days, vowing to keep your opinions to yourself in future.

Scenario 7: You've just been promoted.

- **Option 1:** You feel elated, knowing your hard work has paid off and your promotion is well deserved.
- **Option 2:** You feel anxious, worrying that the additional responsibility will be too much and fearing that you might be exposed as an imposter.

Scenario 8: Your colleague has just received the promotion you were hoping for. How do you react?

- **Option 1:** You feel disappointed but acknowledge that they deserved it. You now have a clear idea of what you need to do to secure the promotion next time.
- **Option 2:** You feel devastated, questioning where you went wrong and how you failed to secure the promotion.

Scenario 9: You've just completed a project but haven't received feedback from the project manager.

- **Option 1:** You feel reassured, trusting that the silence means you did a good job. In fact, you're confident in your own performance.
- **Option 2:** You feel uneasy, assuming that no feedback means you've done something wrong and that you've been overlooked.

Scenario 10: It's your grandmother's big birthday celebration, and you need to leave work on time. Just as you're about to leave, your manager asks you to stay late to finish urgent work.

- **Option 1:** You feel disappointed but try to find a solution, considering whether someone else can help or if you can come in early tomorrow.
- **Option 2:** You feel trapped, unable to choose between disappointing your manager or missing your grandmother's celebration.

How did you score?

- If you predominantly selected Option 1, you are likely to already possess a high level of confidence.
- If you mostly selected Option 2, it suggests that you may lack confidence in certain situations. Don't worry—this book is designed to help you build the confidence you need to succeed.

3.02 First Impressions

First impressions are the instantaneous judgements that you make about other people – and they make about you – when you meet them for the first time. While you might think you don't make first impressions, or you try not to, let's do a quick activity to demonstrate that you do make snap judgements about people, even if you don't know why or how.

Activity 5: Snap Judgements

Imagine you're at work and you're about to interview potential candidates for the vacant position in your team—a person with whom you'll be working very closely once appointed. You see a list of candidates and do a quick internet search to see what they look like. The pictures below are those that appear. While you try not to let their pictures influence you in any way, what does your gut reaction tell you? If you were completely honest with yourself, who would you like to be hired? What are your initial thoughts based on these pictures?

How quickly did you make up your mind about who you chose, and how and why did you decide against the other candidates?

In all honesty, it doesn't really matter who you chose. What *does* matter, though, is that you consciously experienced the process your brain goes through when it first meets people. Let's find out what happens.

3.03 Why You Judge People

Research suggests that a single glance of a person's face for just one-tenth of a second is sufficient to form a first impression. That's less time than it takes to click your fingers. Within this fraction of a second, you unconsciously make judgements on a lot of different characteristics, including attractiveness, likeability, trustworthiness, competence, and aggressiveness. In his excellent book, *Face Value*, Professor of Psychology Alexander Todorov says:

> *"We presented our participants with faces flashed for 100 milliseconds (one-tenth of a second), 500 milliseconds, or a full second [...] We thought that people would be able to make such character judgements as trustworthiness, aggressiveness, and competence only after longer presentation of the faces. After all, one-tenth of a second is just one-tenth of a second. We were wrong. One-tenth of a second of viewing provided ample face information for our participants to make up their minds. The effect of additional time was to simply increase confidence in their judgements."*[7]

You make up your mind about someone—whether you like and trust them, for example—almost instantly. This happens beyond your conscious awareness, meaning that first impressions must be formed by System 1. It is System 1's job to keep you safe by constantly scanning the environment for danger, even beyond your conscious awareness. Its role in keeping you safe includes System 1 making instantaneous judgements about other people. This ability is believed to have evolved as a survival mechanism: if our cave-dwelling

---

[7] Todorov, A. (2017) *Face Value: the irresistible influence of first impressions.* Princeton University Press.

ancestors encountered a stranger, they had a split second to decide whether that person was a friend or foe. If they got it wrong, it could have been fatal; if they got it right, they would have survived and passed on their ability to read others correctly to their offspring.

When you meet someone new, your System 1 makes a decision about them before you've even had time to consciously think about or rationalise your assumptions—all in the name of protecting you from harm.

This automatic process explains why you instinctively form opinions about people's likeability, trustworthiness, and confidence with just a glance. Activity 5, which you completed earlier, was designed to help you *feel* System 1 in action as it prompted you to make snap judgements about the individuals you observed.

This can explain why you might have a gut feeling—positive or negative—about someone you've just met, but can't always explain *why* you feel that way. Of course, the strength of your impression depends on the impact the person makes on you. Most of the time, first impressions will be fairly innocuous, leaving you with a slightly positive or slightly negative feeling. But there will be times when you experience a strong positive or negative reaction, and this can be cause for concern due to the long-term consequences.

Here's the key takeaway: other people are doing the exact same thing to you when they meet you for the first time. Understanding why you make snap judgements is just the beginning. To truly appreciate the enormous power of first impressions on the Success Cycle, we need to delve deeper into the science of how your mind interacts with the outside world.

3.04 How Your Mind Filters The World

To understand how your mind processes information and then forms first impressions, we need to look at a pivotal model called the NLP Communication model. This model is borrowed from the field of Neuro Linguistic Programming (NLP).

The NLP Communication Model can be represented by this illustration:

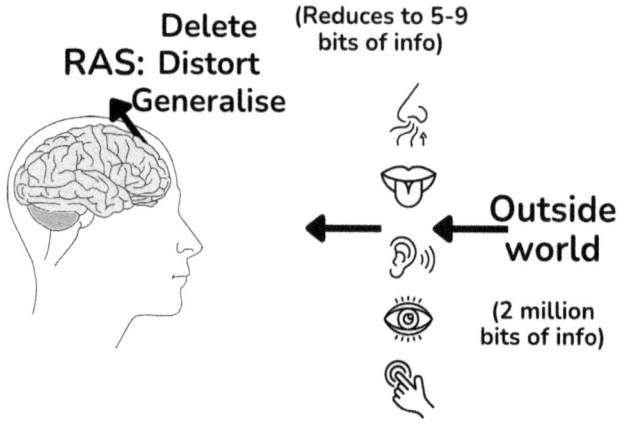

The model was developed by John Grinder and Richard Bandler, the co-creators of NLP, to explain how we, as human beings, take information from the outside world into our brains.[8]

The illustration shows that your five senses—sight, sound, smell, taste, and touch—take in the external events happening around you—an incredible two million bits of information per second. All of these bits of information are then passed through a powerful filtering system to reduce them to a number that System 2 can cope with. This is roughly five to nine *chunks* of information per second.[9]

Before moving on, let's clarify what we mean by 'chunks'. When you learn a new piece of information, like a long list of groceries, for example, you don't memorise each individual item one by one. Instead, you group them into chunks—such as vegetables, dairy products, and snacks—because it's easier to remember and process. If someone lists the groceries differently, such as grouping all items

---

[8] *The model as presented here is a slightly simplified version of the original so that we can focus on the key elements relevant to this book.*

[9] *This is according to research carried out by the American psychologist George Miller who published a paper in 1956 in the journal Psychological Review called 'The Magical Number Seven, Plus or Minus Two: Some Limits on Our Capacity for Processing Information'. It has been interpreted to argue that the number of objects an average human can hold in their short-term memory is between 5-9 chunks of information.*

randomly, you're likely to get confused because it disrupts the chunks you've already organised. This is a critical point: System 2 is limited in how much it can process at once. It can handle more if the information is chunked together, which allows you to process it more efficiently.

This is why people with good memories often use a technique called the 'method of loci', or the 'memory palace'. The idea is to create a mental map of a familiar space—like a room in your house—and associate pieces of information with specific locations within that room. For example, you might place a loaf of bread on the kitchen table, a bottle of milk in the fridge, and a bunch of bananas on the counter surface. When you need to recall the items, you mentally walk through the room, retrieving each item as you go along. By organising information into chunks and linking them to vivid, memorable locations, it makes it possible to process and recall much more than if you were trying to remember each item in isolation.

While an enormous amount of information is constantly coming at you from the outside world, your brain has an incredible filtering system called the Reticular Activating System (RAS). Its job is to reduce this data into just 5 to 9 manageable chunks. It does this by deleting, generalising, and distorting information to ensure that you are only consciously aware of the things that are important to you (and your survival). System 1, the automatic, unconscious part of your brain, carries out this filtering process to protect System 2—your conscious, logical thinking brain—from mental overload. Understanding how this process of deletion, generalisation, and distortion works is essential before we dive into the impact of first impressions on the Success Cycle. Let's begin with deletion.

3.05 How Your Mind Deletes The World

Deletion is the process by which you selectively pay attention to certain aspects of your experience and exclude others. Do the following activity to experience deletion in action.

Activity 6: Deletion

Read the following sentence:

"The red sports car speeds past the green bungalow, where a brown-and-white spotted dog is yapping furiously at a passing cyclist wearing purple Lycra shorts. The dog's owner simply smiles because she's happy that the white fluffy clouds have passed, leaving the bright yellow sun shining in the powder-blue sky."

1. After reading the sentence, close your eyes (or look away from the page for a moment). While you do so, try to recall all the instances of the colour red in the sentence.

2. Can you remember what colour the house was? What about the colour of the dog or the cyclist's clothing?

3. Chances are, when you focused on the colour 'red', your brain 'deleted' the other details, like the colour of the house, the cyclist, or the dog. It naturally prioritised the task of finding 'red' and ignored the rest.

You could think of your brain like an internet search engine. If you type 'Porsche' into the search bar, the engine will find everything related to that brand of car—911, Macan, Cayenne, Panamera, and more. What it will not show you are other makes of cars. It's the same with your brain. Once you make your brain aware of Porsches—or the colour red—your Reticular Activating System (RAS) will delete all other cars (colours) and make you consciously aware of Porsches.

The reality is that the Porsches were always there; it's just that, until that moment, you hadn't told your brain they were important to you. So, your RAS deleted them from your conscious awareness.

The brain doesn't do this to trick you—it does it to protect you. Its primary function is survival. By focusing your attention on what's most important and deleting irrelevant information, it ensures you don't become overwhelmed. This is why, when you focus on something new—like a car you've just decided to buy—you suddenly start noticing that same car everywhere. It's not magic; it's just your brain's way of filtering out information that's relevant to you.

As we progress through this book, the significance of this deletion process will become clearer. Understanding how your brain filters information will help you make better decisions, focus on what's important, and avoid distractions. Now let's look at generalisation.

3.06 How Your Mind Generalises The World

Generalisation occurs when a single experience shapes our expectations about an entire category of experiences. This mental shortcut helps us process information efficiently, but it can also lead to assumptions that may not always be accurate. Try the following activity to see generalisation in action.

Activity 7: Generalisation in Action

Read the following sentence carefully:

"Amelia went to a restaurant, looked at the menu, ordered her meal, ate her food, paid the bill, and left."

Now, answer these questions *without looking back at the sentence*:

- What kind of restaurant was it?
- What food did Amelia order?
- Did she eat alone or with others?
- How did she pay—cash or card?
- Did she leave a tip?

1. **Reflect on your answers:**

You likely made assumptions based on your past experiences with restaurants. Perhaps you imagined a fancy restaurant or a casual café. Maybe you pictured

Amelia eating pasta or a burger, paying with a card, or leaving a tip—even though none of these details were actually mentioned.

Why Does This Happen?

Your brain fills in missing details by drawing from previous experiences. This allows you to process new information quickly and efficiently. For example, once you learn that a switch on the wall turns on a light, you automatically assume that other similar-looking switches will function the same way. You don't have to relearn this concept every time—you simply generalise based on past experience.

Without generalisation, navigating daily life would be incredibly challenging. Imagine having to re-learn how to interact in a restaurant, drive a car, or use a smartphone every single time! However, while generalisation is helpful, it can also lead to misunderstandings, stereotypes, or rigid thinking.

For example, after just one experience, you might form sweeping generalisations like:

- *"It always rains in Cornwall."*
- *"People with a high IQ have no common sense."*
- *"Salespeople are fake."*
- *"Politicians are liars."*
- *"Americans are exuberant."*
- *"Brits are reserved."*

While generalisation helps us make sense of the world, it's important to recognise when it leads to inaccurate assumptions. Being aware of this mental process allows us to challenge our biases, question stereotypes, and stay open to new experiences. Let's now turn our attention to distortion.

3.07 How Your Mind Distorts The World

Distortion refers to the way your mind reshapes experiences to align with your existing ideas, perceptions, or emotions. This process can influence how you interpret situations, often reinforcing preconceived notions—whether positive or negative.

For example, imagine you struggle with self-doubt and often question your abilities. You've just had your yearly appraisal, during which your boss highlighted many things you did well and mentioned a couple of areas for improvement. Objectively, it was a balanced and constructive review. However, as you leave the meeting, you feel frustrated and disheartened. Why? Because instead of focusing on the praise and recognition you received, your mind latches onto the critical feedback. You replay those few improvement points over and over, convincing yourself that you're not good enough or that your boss is disappointed in you.

In reality, your boss's feedback was likely meant to help you grow, not to undermine you. But because your self-doubt is already present, your brain distorts the experience to fit that narrative.

Distortion doesn't just work negatively: it can also cause people to interpret situations in an overly optimistic or unrealistic way. An overconfident employee might downplay constructive criticism, dismissing valuable feedback that could help them improve.

This tendency to reshape reality can affect everything from professional relationships to workplace performance and decision-making. Understanding how distortion works can help you recognise when your mind is twisting reality, allowing you to challenge your assumptions and view situations more objectively.

You might be wondering how all of this is relevant to first impressions. Let's find out!

3.08 How First Impressions Shape Success

When you meet someone for the first time, they will delete, distort and generalise all subsequent information about you either positively or negatively depending on whether you made a good or bad first impression. If you create a positive impression, it's as if you can do nothing wrong. If you create a negative impression, however, it's as if you can do nothing right.

Essentially, the first impression you make on another person can determine your long-term success with them.

Recent studies suggest that first impressions aren't even changed by objective facts—in other words, according to the Society for Personality and Social Psychology, 'first impressions are so powerful that they can override what we are told about people.' [10] So, even if your boss introduces you to a new client as the next superstar, you still have to make a good first impression for those words to matter—for that client to believe those words for themselves. (Notice that this is what Sam experienced in her meeting with Frank.) The positive side of this, however, is that if you instantly impress a stranger who's heard negative things about you from someone else, the negative gossip won't make a difference to their first impression of you.

Mental Shortcuts

Why does your mind place so much weight on first impressions? The answer lies in heuristics—the 'mental shortcuts' that we use to help us make decisions. One of the most powerful mental shortcuts is one called *What You See Is All There Is* (WYSIATI) —the idea that when the mind makes a decision, it deals only in 'known knowns' and largely ignores facts that might make the decision more complex. According to Nobel Prize-winner, psychologist, and author of *Thinking Fast and Slow*, Daniel Kahneman, 'System 1 is radically insensitive to both the quality and the quantity of the information that gives rise to impressions and intuitions.'

This process is also known as the 'halo and horns effect'. When we meet someone, and the first impression is positive, we tend to ignore any negative characteristics in them that may emerge later, and focus only on the positive characteristics: we see the person in the 'halo' of

---

[10] *Press Office. (2014). Even Fact Will Not Change First Impressions. Society for Personality and Social Psychology (SPSP) https://www.spsp.org/news-center/press-releases/even-fact-will-not-change-first-impressions*

that positive first impression. It is similar to 'confirmation bias', whereby we confirm what we first think of someone by deleting, distorting and generalising the information available.

On the other hand, when we meet someone and our first impression is negative, we tend to ignore any positive characteristics that might come to light later and focus only on the negative ones. This is the 'horns' effect. For example, you will interpret everything that your new boss does as either positive or negative depending on whether your initial thoughts about him or her were positive or negative. But the question is: how accurate are your instincts?

In his book *Face Value*, Alexander Todorov says:

> 'Putting aside that the majority of recent studies on accuracy rely on still images of faces, many of these studies seem to find evidence that first impressions are accurate.'[11]

So, it would seem that the first impressions people make can indeed be accurate. But what about if you started off on the wrong foot? Can you change someone's opinion of you?

Second Chance

The short answer is: yes, it is possible. But it takes a lot of hard work and consistent effort, unless the circumstances are extreme.

Psychologist Melissa Ferguson from Cornell University says, 'A single piece of extremely negative information undoes a positive first impression but it takes a lot more—like doing something heroic—to overcome a negative first impression.'

For her studies, Ferguson introduces a fictional character (Bob) to subjects. Sometimes, Bob is portrayed as good: he helps a woman carry groceries, he donates time to a soup kitchen, and he gives a ride to a friend. When subjects find out he is convicted of a heinous act involving a child, the good impression of Bob completely flips. Other times, Bob does a hundred things that make subjects see him as a

---

[11] Todorov, A. (2017) Face Value: the irresistible influence of first impressions. Princeton University Press.

moderately nasty guy: he hunts deer out of season, he yells at his girlfriend in public, and he refuses to help a child fix a bike. Then it is revealed that Bob donated a kidney to a stranger. Ferguson's subjects adjusted their opinion: they thought better of him, but they still did not think well of him.[12]

Ultimately, because your first impressions are created by System 1, you have to override them with System 2. And this takes effort—unless an extreme reason lies behind why you might have got your snap judgement wrong. This is great news if you are willing to put in the effort for other people, but it's not so great news if they are unwilling to put in the conscious effort required to change their first impressions of *you*.

The bottom line is that you must create the best possible—most confident—first impression when meeting someone for the first time. Doing so will help your Success Cycle flow in a positive direction, increasing your chances of achieving your goals. In the next chapter, you'll learn exactly how to do this. But what can you do if you've started off on the wrong foot? The answer is: it depends how badly you messed up, and whether you want them to change their mind about you. It's likely that you don't make a hugely positive or hugely negative impression on people when you first meet them, so logic would suggest that you won't have to work hugely hard to change their minds about you.

However, let's suppose that you really messed up and your card has been marked: no matter what you do, you can't get them to change their mind about you. What can you do?

Unless you can do something powerful to change someone's mind, there's very little you *can* do. But it's important to highlight that there will always be people who won't like you (and vice versa), and you have to decide if that's okay or not. You are not always going to gel with everyone: the world is full of unique people with different characters and personalities who—through no one's fault—might not get on. (*The Courage to be Disliked* by Fumitake Koga and Ichiro

---

[12] Weintraub, P. (2015). *The 10-Second Take. Psychology Today.* https://www.psychologytoday.com/us/articles/201511/the-10-second-take

Kishima says that what people think of you is not your 'task': you can only focus on what you can do. So, if you are particularly concerned about what people think of you, I would recommend reading this book.)

The challenge comes when the person who doesn't like you is your manager, and they're making your life hell, or holding you back in some way. If you've tried everything to talk to them and to address their concerns about you, yet they're not willing to budge, you might have to admit defeat and move on. However, it's important to realise that their dislike of you probably reveals more about them than it does about you.

Alternatively, there is the possibility that—beyond first impressions—your behaviour towards them is causing them to react negatively to you. You will learn more about this in Chapter 5.

Before you move onto the next chapter, where you will learn self-coaching strategies for ensuring that you create the best possible first impression of yourself by being your most confident and professional self, it is useful to find out how people see you now so you know where you might like to focus your energy.

3.09 What First Impression Do You make?

Asking a complete stranger to provide an honest appraisal of their first impression of you might prove difficult, so a more direct route is to ask people you already know.

Activity 8: Honest Appraisal

Ask three colleagues—ideally at different levels of seniority—how they think you come across, particularly when meeting new people. Request that they provide some detail in terms of what it is you do that causes them to say that. Request that they are as honest as they can be with you. In return, accept what they say graciously, regardless of whether it's positive or negative: it could transform your career if you choose to listen to their views. If you don't think that they will be honest with you, you could ask for feedback to be given anonymously.

Reflection: What insights have you gained from your colleagues' feedback? (For example: Is it what you were expecting? Is there anything you weren't expecting?)

Activity 8 - Sam's Answer:

Colleague one says: "Sam is highly capable, extremely organised, and efficient. She's also one of the hardest workers I know and is one of the most talented co-ordinators I've had the pleasure of working with; she's particularly brilliant at finding innovative solutions to seemingly impossible challenges. Unfortunately, she doesn't give this highly capable impression to new clients. She avoids eye contact, focuses too much attention on taking notes, and doesn't take the time to build rapport with the other person. For example, she is excellent at driving task-driven discussions, but abruptly steers away from any chit chat, which can give the impression that she's not interested in them. By only showing interest in the task—and not the person—as well her lack of making eye contact and her focus on taking notes, she also gives the impression of being far more junior, and less capable and experienced, than she is."

Colleague two says: "Sam is one the most organised and efficient workers on our team. I know I can rely on Sam no matter what. However, she is one of the quieter members of staff and I find her quite difficult to connect with. For example, if I try to make conversation with her, you can tell she is only interested in work because you get one-word answers while she stares at the screen while trying to avoid eye contact."

Colleague three says: "While Sam is one of the hardest workers I know, and is clearly good at the technical side of her job, she has a big flaw which is that she doesn't stand up for herself. I see people taking advantage of her because they know she won't say 'no' or push back. As a result, she's overloaded with too much work and is always busy and stressed. Her lack of confidence and resilience makes me worry that her promotion to team leader was premature as I find myself doubting her ability to lead others when she can barely keep on top of her own workload."

Sam's thoughts:

"I'm really taken aback. While I appreciate they've said some positive things about my work, they've said some really negative things about me. The thing that upsets me the most is that people think I'm quiet and difficult to connect with. Davide (my partner) would laugh out loud if he knew that's what my colleagues said about me! I am the talkative one in our family, known as the joker who loves to have fun. How can they have such a wrong impression of me? I'm mortified.

It would also seem that they think others take advantage of me because I can't say 'no'. I thought I was being nice and helpful but now it would seem they think I'm a pushover! Davide would laugh at this too because he says I'm bossy! I hate that some people doubt my ability to lead because this doesn't bode well for me to be a Project Manager. When I also factor in Frank's comments that he thought I was more junior and less experienced than I am, it's clear that I'm definitely not giving off the right impression of myself."

Chapter Summary

As a human being, your System 1 instinctively judges strangers almost instantaneously through first impressions. These initial impressions—shaped by the *halo and horns effect*—play a crucial role in determining your long-term success with another person. While you can actively engage System 2 to override any unconscious biases you may have about others, the challenge is that you cannot rely on others to do the same for you.

This makes it essential to understand how you come across, especially when meeting people for the first time. By projecting confidence, you can ensure that your actions steer the Success Cycle in a positive direction—one that creates favourable outcomes for you. Otherwise, you risk unintentionally giving the wrong impression and setting the cycle in the wrong direction.

What's Next?

The next chapter provides top tips and practical strategies to help you consciously engage System 2 and project confidence. By doing so, you'll create the best possible first impression, ensuring the Success Cycle moves in a direction that helps you achieve your goals.

BUILDING OUTER CONFIDENCE: ESSENTIAL SKILLS FOR PRESENCE AND IMPACT

"The only thing you should be faking is confidence. If you don't have it yet, pretend that you do. Pretend you're not nervous, pretend you're not scared, and after a while, the pretend part disappears."
Patricia V Davis [13]

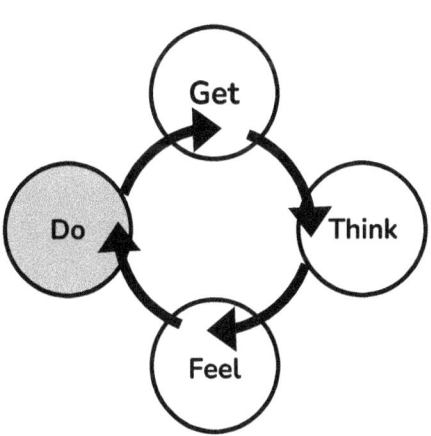

There is little doubt that Sam is highly capable and experienced in her job, and she is recognised for this by the

---

[13] *Patricia V. Davis is an American novelist and non-fiction writer.*

people who know her well and work with her regularly. If this wasn't the case, she wouldn't have been promoted to team leader. But when it comes to people who don't know her well, there is a mismatch between who she really is on the inside (experienced, capable, fun and chatty) and how she is perceived on the outside (inexperienced, incapable, transactional and quiet).

In terms of how this impacts the Success Cycle, Sam's behaviour (what she does) is holding her back from getting what she wants: a promotion. The good news is that Sam is not in conscious control of her behaviour—yet. So, when she chooses to, she can consciously engage System 2 to change what she does to bring it more in line with who she really is. In this way, she can give herself more of a chance of getting what she wants. (In Part Three, you'll find out how she can be more of who she is without having to make a consistent, conscious effort.)

This chapter focuses on what you can do consciously to project confidence, even in moments of doubt or discomfort. By engaging System 2 thinking, you'll learn self-coaching techniques to fine-tune your verbal and nonverbal behaviours, ensuring you make a strong and positive impression. These small, intentional adjustments will help you appear more self-assured and in control, even when you don't necessarily feel that way inside. As a result, you'll be able to 'fake it until you make it' with purpose. Through practical strategies and self-discipline, you'll develop the ability to manage your presence in high-stakes situations, such as meetings or networking events. By the end, you'll have a personalised self-coaching plan to build confidence daily and turn the Success Cycle in your favour.

What This Chapter Covers:

- 4.01 Appearance
- 4.02 Posture
- 4.03 Smile

- 4.04 Eye contact
- 4.05 Gestures
- 4.06 Pace
- 4.07 Pitch
- 4.08 Filler words

4.01 Appearance

Appearance can include a whole host of things: your clothes, shoes, hair, make-up, jewellery, teeth, glasses, tattoos, and piercings, etc. Remember that—rightly or wrongly—people make generalisations based on your appearance, so make sure you consciously pick attire that lets other people know who you are while helping you achieve what you want. In short, make sure that your conscious choice of appearance means that people make the right generalisations about you.

Most companies have a dress code policy, so this is your best guide to ensuring you make the right impression. Even if you look immaculate, however, antiquated social prejudices could still cause you problems—rightly or wrongly—so you might like to understand how these can impact how others view you, and treat you.

> **EXAMPLE: WRONG KIND OF ATTENTION**
>
> Many years ago, a delegate on one of my courses looked incredibly smart. She wore a tailored suit and blouse, her shoes were shiny, and her hair, make-up and nails looked like she'd just walked out of a salon. In essence, she was a beautiful woman who was immaculately turned out. While she came across as someone who cared about her appearance (something that was important to her), the reason she was on the course was because she wanted to gain respect from her boss and clients. She had been a Personal Assistant for a few years and was frustrated that the middle-aged senior executives she had to deal with were more concerned with flirting with her than talking to

her—or taking her—seriously. In her words, "They talk to me like I'm an airhead and I've had enough. I want to move to the next level but no one takes me seriously."

While there was little doubt her appearance was immaculate, there was also little doubt that her skirt was *very* short, her blouse was *very* low cut and her heels were incredibly high. While she *should* have been able to wear what she felt comfortable in, we discussed the potential impression she might be giving off and why it might produce the outcome she gets. She admitted that being well turned out was hugely important to her, but she realised her outfit might be giving off certain vibes to certain sectors of the organisation. So she wondered if a few modifications might help her to be taken more seriously.

The following day, she arrived with a knee-length skirt and a blouse that reached her neckline but she wore the same six inch shoes. She was still immaculately turned out and felt like she was still herself at work, but her outfit conveyed a different impression of herself. She contacted me weeks later to say that her boss and clients had started taking her more seriously.

Equally, not taking care of your appearance can also give off the wrong impression of you, your work ethic *and* the organisation for which you work.

EXAMPLE: YOU REFLECT YOUR WORK AND THE ORGANISATION

A different delegate on another course turned up in a faded suit that was a size too small for him, a creased shirt, and scuffed shoes. His hair also looked like it hadn't been brushed in a very long time. It appeared that he didn't care about the way he looked. As an employee of a professional services firm, his manager felt too uncomfortable sending him to meet with clients, which should have been a large part of his role, because she was concerned that they would think his work, and the organisation, were as shoddy as his appearance.

On the course, it became obvious very quickly that he didn't realise there was anything wrong with the way he looked because he didn't pay much heed to such frivolous matters: he was just interested in the quality of his work. Again, whether he was right or wrong is not for this book. What was important, however, was that he felt frustrated about not being sent out to meet with clients.

I had a quiet chat with him and suggested he buy a new suit that fitted him (or a second hand one if he couldn't afford a brand new one), that he should iron his shirt, and if he couldn't afford a new pair of shoes, to at least polish the ones he had. Finally, I suggested a haircut or a thorough comb through.

When a dapper, smart and well-turned-out man arrived the next day, the rest of the delegates and I couldn't take our eyes off him. We were all blown away by the transformation! It was amazing how a change of clothes and a haircut could make someone look more confident, professional and mature. Interestingly, he even commented that he felt more confident too. His manager was more than happy to send him out to a client site the very next day.

Of course, anyone *should* be able to wear anything of their choosing, but there are (sadly) some generalisations that—rightly or wrongly—create certain impressions. And unless you are aware of what you look like and how it could be perceived, it's difficult to know what it is that is holding you back from getting what you want. If you are brave enough, ask friends and colleagues to provide feedback on your appearance, and what it says about you.

4.02 Posture

Standing tall, pulling your shoulders back, and holding your head straight are all signs of confidence and competence, so why not do these things too? This doesn't change who you are: you're simply changing your body to appear confident. And remember: confidence is just a behaviour that can become a skill through practise, which means that anyone can learn to look and sound like a confident person by changing their body language, voice and choice of words. (This is different to *being* a confident person or someone who is fearless and believes they can succeed at anything. We'll cover how to achieve this in Part Three.)

Amy Cuddy's concept of the *power pose* popularised the idea that standing confidently can actually make you feel more confident. This supports the notion that the body influences the mind, meaning you can use your physicality to trigger physiological changes. (Cuddy's research found that a two minute 'power pose' caused an increase in the levels of testosterone and a decrease in the levels of cortisol, or the stress hormone, in the brain.) [14]

While her research has faced criticism, there's little doubt that the way you sit or stand affects how you feel. If you slouch, roll your shoulders forward, and look down, you're more likely to feel unconfident. On the other hand, standing tall with your shoulders back and looking straight ahead can not only make you *appear* more confident to others but can also boost how confident you *feel*. However, be mindful that this effect is temporary: once you stop *power posing*, your body stops producing those confidence-boosting hormones, bringing you back to where you started.

In Part Three, you'll learn how to build lasting confidence from within, without relying on external techniques. In the meantime, these quick fixes can help you adjust your body language to project confidence in the moment.

4.03 Smile

A smile can put others at ease by making you appear friendly and approachable. Research has even shown that people who smile regularly can appear more confident, which can mean they are more likely to be promoted[15].

---

[14] Nison, M. (2012). It only takes 2 minutes in a 'power pose' to completely boost confidence. Insider. https://www.businessinsider.com/harvard-amy-cuddy-power-pose-research-2012-10

[15] Stibich, M. (2021). Top 10 Reasons to Smile Every Day. Very Well Mind. https://www.verywellmind.com/top-reasons-to-smile-every-day-2223755

In addition to helping you come across as friendly, approachable and confident, smiling can impact how you feel too. According to an article in *Psychology Today*,[16] smiling activates the release of tiny molecules called neuropeptides, which help to reduce stress. (Neuropeptides help our nervous system to send messages throughout our bodies, and those signals vary according to our emotional state—be that happy, sad, angry, depressed, or excited.) So-called 'feel-good' signalling molecules—dopamine, endorphins and serotonin—are also released when you smile; they act to relax your body, and can also lower your heart rate and blood pressure. (This is an example of how the different elements of the Success Cycle can impact each other—that is, how what you do can influence how you feel, as well as the other way round.)

So, a simple smile can make all the difference to how you come across, and it can make you feel happier too. And the best thing about it is that it's free!

4.04 Eye contact

As well as making you appear confident, looking someone in the eye shows that you are listening to them, that you care about them, and you are interested in what they're saying. It shows that you value and respect them. Conversely, if you don't look someone in the eye, it can make you look shifty, or shy.

A 2007 study led by Loyola Marymount University professor Nora A. Murphy found that looking your conversation partner in the eye was huge for your perceived smartness. "Looking while speaking was a key behaviour," Murphy wrote. "It significantly correlated with IQ, was successfully manipulated by impression-managing targets, and contributed to higher perceived intelligence ratings." Wearing thick glasses and speaking expressively helps too. [17]

So, looking others in the eye can help you appear more confident, and can also help others to think that you're interested in them too.

---

[16] Stevenson, S. (2012). *There's Magic in Your Smile*. Psychology Today. https://www.psychologytoday.com/us/blog/cutting-edge-leadership/201206/there-s-magic-in-your-smile

[17] Murphy, N. (2007). *Appearing Smart*. National Library of Medicine. https://pubmed.ncbi.nlm.nih.gov/17312315/

4.05 Gestures

Gestures are the movements you make with your body and can include your hands and facial expressions (which also include smiling and eye contact; see above). Gestures are activated automatically when you speak because it's a natural form of non-verbal communication that builds trust and emphasises what you say. According to research carried out on the body language of TED Talk speakers, it was discovered that the more hand gestures, the more successful the Talk! The research found that there was a direct correlation between the number of views of a TED Talk and the number of hand gestures: 18 minute TED Talks that used an average of 272 hand gestures attracted an average of 124,000 views; by contrast, TED Talks that used an average of 465 hand gestures attracted an average of 7,360,000 views. So, nearly double the number of hand gestures increased views by a factor of almost 60![18]

Why is this? Holler and Beatie[19] found that gestures increase the value of the spoken message by sixty per cent. It's believed that, in addition to showing and building trust, hand gestures emphasise the important points someone is making.

However, gestures can either increase or decrease trust and understanding depending on the level of something called congruency. Congruency is achieved when your non-verbal communication matches your verbal communication; incongruency occurs when your body language and voice do not match what you say. You might have experienced this yourself when you have asked a colleague to do something, and while they said that they would do it, you didn't believe that they would. It's likely that you noticed—consciously or unconsciously—a disconnect between what they said, and how they said it. This is because we only believe what people say

---

[18] Van Edwards, V. 5 secrets of a successful TED Talk. Science of People https://www.scienceofpeople.com/secrets-of-a-successful-ted-talk/

[19] Holler, J., & Geoffrey, B. (2007). Gesture use in social interaction: how speakers' gestures can reflect listeners' thinking. In L. Mondada (Ed.), On-line Proceedings of the 2nd Conference of the International Society of Gesture Studies, Lyon, France 15-18 June 2005.

when *what* they say is matched with *how* they say it (and their associated behaviour).

To understand why this is so, let's look at a commonly-cited psychology study released in 1967, which was carried out by Albert Mehrabian at UCLA[20]. The study examined what happens when there is incongruency between the three key areas of human communication: words, voice and facial expressions. For example, when someone's voice tone, facial expressions and words don't match, which do you believe? The conclusions of his study were as follows:

- 7% of the message pertaining to feelings and attitudes is in the words that are spoken.

- 38% of the message pertaining to feelings and attitudes is conveyed in the way that the words are said i.e. the tone of voice.

- 55% of the message pertaining to feelings and attitudes is conveyed in the facial expression used.

The following pie chart illustrates these results.

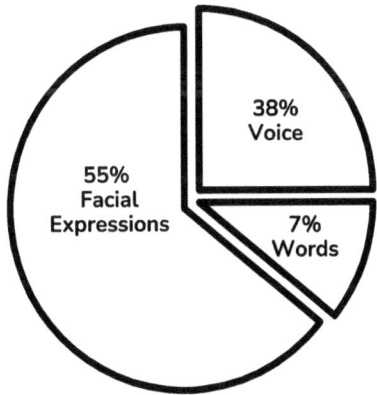

What Mehrabian's study shows is that when the non-verbal clues (tone of voice and facial expressions) don't match the verbal clues (the

---

[20] Chapman, A. (2017). *Mehrabian's Communications Theory: verbal, non-verbal, body language.* Business Balls. https://www.businessballs.com/communication-skills/mehrabians-communication-theory-verbal-non-verbal-body-language/

words) of someone communicating their feelings, the other person will believe the non-verbal clues more than the verbal clues. This means that if you say the word "no" but your non-verbal clues don't back it up—like speaking quickly and avoiding eye contact—others will likely doubt you really mean it.

Ultimately, what this means is that you need to use your gestures as you normally and naturally would. If you don't, you could risk invalidating your message and achieving the opposite of what you want.

Some people gesture much more than others. In terms of the amount of gesturing *you* should do to appear more confident, it's about being your authentic self as much as possible. One suggestion is to become aware of what your facial expressions and hand gestures do when you feel comfortable and replicate them consciously when you feel uncomfortable.

Continuing with the theme of congruency, it's important to support congruency by both looking and *sounding* confident too. So, how can we do this?

4.06 Pace

According to a study published in the Journal of Personality and Social Psychology in the 1970s, people who talked at a moderately fast pace (195 words per minute) were found to be more intelligent, persuasive, credible, and socially-attractive, whereas those who talked more slowly (100 words per minute or less) were found to be less intelligent and credible. So, what is the optimal rate at which to speak? A 2011 study conducted by researchers at the University of Michigan sought to answer exactly this question. They found that the sweet spot for success was a moderately fast 210 words per minute—anything higher or lower than this was not as effective.

So, if you want to come across as confident then you want to speak at roughly 210 words per minute. One way to practise this could be to spend time reading out loud and focusing on every word. This technique forces you to speak clearly and include natural pauses, both of which are great for sounding genuine. When you get a good rhythm going, slowly build up your speaking rate until you hit the optimum level[21].

4.07 Pitch

Researchers at McMaster University in Canada, led by Cara Tigue, have studied perceptions of vocal pitch. She and her team asked 125 people to listen to nine US presidents, going back to Harry Truman, to judge higher and lower pitched versions of their voices. In all cases, they voted for the deeper tones.[22] Overall, the researchers found that voters prefer lower-pitched voices, rating their speakers higher for attractiveness, leadership potential, honesty, intelligence and dominance. Tigue says:

> "Throughout our evolutionary history, it would have been important for our ancestors to pay attention to cues to good leadership because group leaders affected a person's ability to survive and reproduce within a group...We're looking at it in a present-day, twenty-first-century context."

In another study carried out in 2012, researchers at the University of Miami and Duke University asked people to listen to recordings of men and women saying "I urge you to vote for me this November." Results showed that participants were more likely to say they'd vote for females with lower-pitched voices. That was largely because the females with lower-pitched voices were seen as more competent and trustworthy.[23]

So, if you want to come across as confident, you want to ensure that you lower your tone. This is particularly important if you're female because women, generally, have higher-pitched voices than men.

---

[21] Van Edwards, V. How to speak with confidence and sound better. Blog. Science of People. https://www.scienceofpeople.com/speak-with-confidence/

[22] Martinson, J. (2011). Must a woman lower the tone of her voice to be successful. The Guardian. https://www.theguardian.com/lifeandstyle/the-womens-blog-with-jane-martinson/2011/nov/15/woman-lower-tone-voice-successful.

[23] Klofstad, C. A., Anderson, R.C., Peters, S. (2012) Sounds like a winner: voice pitch influences perception of leadership capacity in both men and women. Proc Biol Sci. doi: 10.1098/rspb.2012.0311.

4.08 Filler Words

Many people use filler words— 'kind of', 'um', 'ah,' 'like', and 'you know'—in everyday conversations. Normally, such words go unnoticed unless a particular word is used excessively. However, if you want to appear confident, filler words can diminish your level of believability and credibility. To appreciate this, compare the following two sentences:

> **Fred:** 'No, I'm, kind of, really sorry but perhaps, maybe, I can't, like, um, do that, um, right, now, like, you know.'
>
> **Freddie:** 'No, I'm sorry but I can't do that right now.'

Who do you believe means 'no'? Who could you persuade to change their stance and agree to what you're asking them to do? Hopefully you've said that Fred used too many filler words, which might lead you to think that you could get him to say 'yes' (and it wouldn't take much persuasion, either), while you would accept that Freddie meant 'no', so you wouldn't bother trying to persuade him otherwise.

If you discover that you use filler words when you feel nervous or stressed, one way to eliminate them is to replace them with a pause instead—an approach that can make you sound more eloquent.

A recent story in the *New York Times*, for example, calls attention to the silence between notes of a piece of classical music, explaining why short pauses draw so much attention. As social beings, we are hard-wired to pay attention to breaks in the flow of communication. "We recognise the pregnant pause, the stunned silence, the expectant hush," the author writes. "A one-beat delay on an answer can reveal hesitation or hurt, or play us for laughs." Pauses are interpreted as eloquence—in music and in public speech.[24]

So, if you perhaps, maybe, use some, kind of, um, filler words, like, you might want to substitute these meaningless expressions for a

---

[24] Gallo, C. (2019). *How to look and sound confident during a presentation*. Harvard Business Review. https://hbr.org/2019/10/how-to-look-and-sound-confident-during-a-presentation

pause instead: not only will you appear more confident and believable, but you'll come across as more eloquent too.

Activity 9: Engage System 2 to Make Intentional Changes to Your Behaviour

In this activity, you'll use deliberate, strategic thinking (System 2) to fine-tune your verbal and non-verbal communication so you can consistently project more confidence in every situation.

1. **Identify key areas for improvement:** Based on your self-analysis and the feedback from colleagues (Activity 8 in the last chapter), choose 2-3 specific areas to focus on. Examples could include:

    - **Posture:** Stand taller and avoid slouching.
    - **Eye contact:** Practice making steady, but natural, eye contact in conversations.
    - **Voice tone:** Work on speaking more clearly and confidently, avoiding filler words like "um" or "like."
    - **Facial expressions:** Smile more often and keep an open, approachable expression.
    - **Attire/grooming:** Opt for clothing that aligns with your professional goals and is clean and well-maintained.

2. **Set a practice routine:**

    - Choose one area to focus on each week. For example, Week 1: Focus on improving posture. Week 2: Work on eye contact, and so on.
    - Implement small daily practices to reinforce these changes (for example, check your posture when walking or standing, practice smiling in the mirror, etc.)

3. **Use System 2 to monitor your progress:**
   - At the end of each week, review how you've implemented the changes.
   - Ask yourself, "Did I notice a difference in how I was perceived in meetings or interactions? Did I feel more confident?"
   - Make necessary adjustments based on these reflections and continue refining your approach.

Activity 9 - Sam's Answer:

"Making eye contact would be a good start for me. That seems to be one of the key things that says to others that I don't have confidence in myself. Also, smiling more and talking to people about things other than work would help. And, although no one commented on it, I know I use a lot of filler words, which make me sound like I lack confidence in what I'm saying. So I really want to focus on cutting these out too. Perhaps I could try using silence instead. This would be particularly useful when I want to share my ideas in meetings, and speak with authority."

Chapter Summary

By harnessing the power of System 2, you can apply proven strategies to project confidence—even when you don't feel it on the inside—while still staying true to yourself. At first, these adjustments may feel unnatural, but they don't change *who* you are: they simply refine *how* you present yourself. This approach won't guarantee that you'll always get what you want—nothing can—but it will significantly improve your ability to create strong first impressions, appear confident at work, and steer the Success Cycle in a direction that works in your favour.

What's Next?

The next chapter explores another key aspect of the *do* part of the Success Cycle: assertiveness. You'll assess how you respond to difficult people and challenging situations, as well as how your behaviour influences the outcomes you achieve (or fail to achieve) at work. By the end of the chapter, you'll gain insights into how your System 1 currently operates on autopilot in professional settings, laying the groundwork for learning how to override it through self-coaching with System 2.

THE SCIENCE OF ASSERTIVENESS: FINDING YOUR VOICE

> *"The difference between successful people and really successful people is that really successful people say no to almost everything."*
> **Warren Buffett**[25]

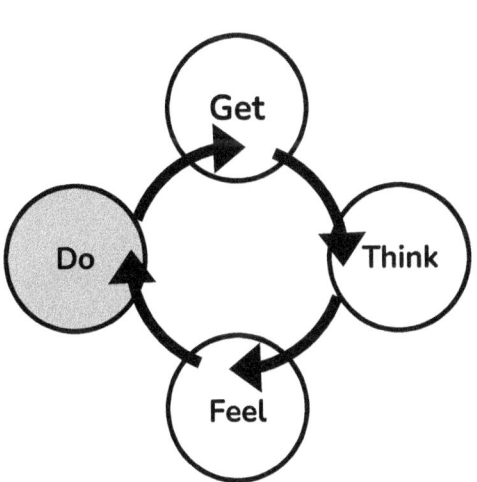

Sam feels relaxed and comfortable with certain people—her brother; her partner, Davide; a few close friends; and some

---

[25] Warren Buffett is an American business magnate, investor, and philanthropist. According to Wikipedia, as of June 2023, he possessed a net worth of $117 billion, making him the fifth-richest person in the world.

colleagues at work. These are people with whom she is able to be her fun, chatty and confident self. She finds that she is happy to talk about anything without fear of reprisal; she also feels able to speak up and share her thoughts and opinions while listening to theirs. She is also more than willing to say 'no' if she doesn't want to do something and she'll challenge them if she doesn't agree with them. In terms of the Success Cycle, this means she's more likely to get what she wants because she's letting others know what she wants.

Sam feels the opposite with certain people at work, especially those with more knowledge, experience, and seniority. When she is with these people, she tenses up and feels uncomfortable, which causes her—unconsciously—to avoid eye contact and steer away from non-work conversations. In terms of the Success Cycle, this means she's unlikely to get what she wants because her colleagues don't know what that is.

While she now has some tools to be able to fake confidence when she is with these people, Sam still needs to learn how to assert herself confidently so she can say 'no' and push back on additional work when necessary.

Are you like Sam, whereby your behaviour changes depending on your mood, the situation, or the person you're interacting with? Perhaps you go quiet with certain people, assertive with others, and even aggressive with specific individuals. Or do you find that you behave in a consistent way with everyone, at every level, and in every situation no matter what?

This chapter explores your behaviour in terms of how you react or respond to the people and situations you have to deal with (i.e. what you do), and how this affects what you get. It reveals four types of behaviours—passive, passive-aggressive, aggressive and assertive— and helps you understand which of these could best help you achieve your objectives so you can get the results you want in your career.

What This Chapter Covers:

- 5.01 Assessing Your Assertiveness
- 5.02 Understanding the Spectrum of Workplace Behaviours
- 5.03 How Behaviour Choices Shape Workplace Dynamics
- 5.04 Why Do People React Non-Assertively?
- 5.05 Non-Assertive Behaviour in Action
- 5.06 What Stops People Being Assertive?
- 5.07 Is Assertiveness Always the Best Option?
- 5.08 Who Are You Non-Assertive With?

5.01 Assessing Your Assertiveness

Let's find out how assertive you currently are in the workplace.

Activity 10: Assessing Your Assertiveness

In the workplace, you'll face challenges that can test your ability to handle difficult situations. Are you able to stand your ground and respond assertively, or do you tend to avoid confrontation, suppress your feelings, or lash out? Let's explore how you behave when faced with challenging circumstances. Your responses can provide insight into your assertiveness levels.

For each scenario, choose the option that most closely reflects how you would react. Keep in mind that this is about how you *currently* respond, not how you *should* respond.

> **Scenario 1:** Your colleague Simon, with whom you frequently work, sends you unsolicited feedback via email. How do you respond?
>
> a). You avoid responding, feel upset, and distance yourself from him. You might gossip about Simon behind his back, criticising him for not delivering the feedback face-to-face.

b). You intentionally exclude him from an important client meeting to subtly get back at him for the email. Later, you claim it was a mistake.

c). You immediately call him, angrily reprimanding him for not giving feedback in person and accusing him of being cowardly.

d). You schedule a meeting with him to discuss the feedback calmly. You ask him to clarify his points, thank him for sharing his thoughts, and express that in the future, you'd prefer feedback to be given in person.

Which response best aligns with your approach?

Scenario 2: A client, who has become too familiar, invites you on a personal outing. You don't want to accept, as it crosses the boundary between professional and personal. How do you handle the situation?

a). You accept the invitation to avoid upsetting the client, or you make up an excuse to decline.

b). You accept but spend the entire time talking about your partner, trying to make it clear that you're in a relationship.

c). You confront the client, telling her that her invitation is inappropriate and that you prefer to maintain professional boundaries.

d). You call her, thanking her for the invitation but seeking clarification on whether it's a professional or personal invitation. Depending on her response, you either accept for professional reasons or politely decline, making it clear that you prefer to keep work and personal life separate.

Which response most closely matches your reaction?

Scenario 3: Your boss, who plays a significant role in your career progression, asks you to stay late again. This is the fourth Friday in a row, and you're frustrated that work is interfering with your personal life. How do you respond?

a). You agree to stay late, although you feel resentful. You vent your frustration privately to a friend afterward.

b). You reluctantly agree but drag your feet, making sure your boss knows that you're unhappy about it.

c). You refuse, telling your boss that you can't continue sacrificing your personal time and suggest a better way to manage workloads.

d). You explain that while you're committed to your work, you also value your personal time. You request a compromise, such as having someone else handle the task or working on it during office hours.

Which response best represents your typical behaviour?

What did your answers reveal about your assertiveness?

- If you answered mostly d), you display strong assertiveness and are likely able to handle challenging situations with clarity and confidence.

- If your responses leaned toward a), b), or c), it suggests that you may struggle with assertiveness in some areas. This is an opportunity to explore how you can be more confident in standing up for yourself.

5.02 Understanding the Spectrum of Workplace Behaviours

The four behaviours that you have at your disposal when interacting with others are: Aggressive, Passive, Passive-Aggressive and Assertive. Below is an overview of each of the behaviours. As you read each description, be curious about which one you think describes your dominant behaviour at work.

Aggressive behaviour is when you...

- Are only concerned with your own needs and getting your own way

- Say your beliefs as if they are facts: 'That won't work' or 'That was stupid'
- Tell others to do something rather than ask them if they would like to do it
- Undermine and criticise others to make yourself feel better
- Put others down to build yourself up
- Do not show praise or your appreciation of others
- Express yourself through insults and sarcasm, as well as hostile statements and actions
- Shout a lot!

In a nutshell, a person exhibits aggressive behaviour when they put their needs before the needs of others, and ensure they get what they want no matter what the consequences for other people. In this way, they win and others lose.

Passive behaviour is when you...

- Ensure everyone else's views and ideas are heard but keep your own views and ideas to yourself
- Respond with 'I don't mind' when asked to express your preference
- Are unable to give a straight answer when you're asked for your opinion
- Are unwilling to speak your truth openly, and honestly
- Procrastinate so that no one will know how afraid you are of being inadequate
- Let other people violate your personal right to be treated with respect.

In short, we see passive behaviour when a person puts other people's needs above their own to ensure others get what they want, no matter the consequences to themselves. As a result, they lose and others win.

Passive-Aggressive behaviour is when you.

- Play mind games and guilt-trip people into doing what you want them to do
- Express hostility in indirect ways, such as sulking or slamming doors
- Do things to spite the other person i.e. be late
- Make up stories, excuses and lies, and spread rumours
- Mask nasty comments by saying 'only joking!' afterwards
- Complain bitterly about someone behind their back, but be nice to their face

We see passive-aggressive behaviour when someone ignores other people's needs and seeks to punish them, no matter the consequences for their own needs. In this way, everyone loses! The well-known phrase 'cut your nose off to spite your face' fits nicely here.

Assertive behaviour is when you...

- Confidently express yourself, and listen to others
- Exercise personal rights without denying the rights of others
- Compromise to reach the best solution for both of you
- Stand up for yourself while respecting the rights of others
- Communicate with others in a direct and honest manner without intentionally hurting their feelings
- Express your thoughts in direct, honest, and appropriate ways that do not violate the rights of others
- Deal with problems directly

In brief, we see assertive behaviour when an individual honours their own needs *and* the needs of other people. They compromise to ensure that the needs of both sides are (mostly) met. In this way, everyone wins!

Now that you have a general overview of the four most common types of behaviour exhibited at work, let's look at what your answers to Activity 10 reveal about how you typically behave at work.

5.03 How Behaviour Choices Shape Workplace Dynamics

Scenario 1: Your colleague Simon, with whom you frequently work, sends you unsolicited feedback via email. How do you respond?

a). You avoid responding, feel upset, and distance yourself from him.

b). You intentionally exclude him from an important client meeting.

c). You immediately call him, angrily reprimanding him.

d). You schedule a meeting with him to discuss the feedback calmly.

Which option did you choose?

If you answered a), this is passive behaviour. The problem with this reaction is that Simon will never know that you were bothered by the way he delivered his feedback. He'll also think that it is an acceptable way to give feedback so he is unlikely to change his behaviour. Your relationship with him might also suffer and you also might cause a divide in the office if your other colleagues feel that they have to choose between you and Simon. This could—potentially—end badly for you.

If you answered b), this is passive-aggressive behaviour. The problem with this reaction is that Simon will know that you did it deliberately, which may lead him to send you further 'developmental' feedback via email, which will wind you up even more. He may also tell colleagues what you did, which might harm your reputation. If your boss finds out, there could be problems for you because they will be annoyed that the client lost out because of a petty spat between you and Simon.

If you answered c), this is aggressive behaviour. The problem with this reaction is that, while you might feel better in the short term (because you've expressed your anger and upset), it will back-fire in the long term. No one wants to work with a bully, and so you might find that Simon avoids you like the plague. If this is how you commonly react at work when things irritate you, you might find that no one wants to work with you, including your boss. Alternatively, Simon might stand up to you and give you a piece of his mind the next time you bump into each other, which could result in a stand-up shouting match in the middle of the office. This is not what your boss would consider team work!

If you answered d), congratulations, this behaviour is assertive! This is the only response that enables you to express your true feelings about being given some feedback that you found difficult to take, especially via email. It is also a good way to be able to discuss the feedback further and talk about why you might have done what you did and why Simon felt the way he did about it, which may help you to learn, grow and develop. Simon will also discover that it is not acceptable to email 'developmental' feedback and would hopefully not do it again to you or anyone else. It shows that you respect yourself and, if Simon has any sense, he will respect you too.

> **Scenario 2:** A client, who has become too familiar, invites you on a personal outing. You don't want to accept, as it crosses the boundary between professional and personal. How do you handle the situation?
>
> a). You accept the invitation to avoid upsetting the client.
>
> b). You accept but spend the entire time talking about your partner.
>
> c). You confront the client, telling her that her invitation is inappropriate.

d). You call her, thanking her for the invitation but seeking clarification on whether it's a professional or personal invitation.

Which option did you choose?

If you answered a), this is passive behaviour. The problem with this reaction is that, if she *has* got personal reasons for asking you, she might take your acceptance of the invitation as proof that the attraction is mutual. This opens you up to more awkward situations in the future. If you lied by saying that you had to work when you didn't, she will ask you again, and there are only so many times that you can use work as an excuse.

If you answered b), this is passive-aggressive behaviour. The problem with this reaction is that you end up ruining the day for you and for her. If it turns out that her intentions were purely professional, then you could damage your relationship: she might not want to work with someone who complains a lot or can't manage their emotions. Even if her intentions were personal, she may know you're lying because your colleague told her you were single, in which case she's not going to trust you on a personal or professional level, so you might find that you have one less client in the future.

If you answered c), this is aggressive behaviour. The problem with this reaction is that, although you get your point across and she knows where you stand, your manner is likely to put her off from wanting any relationship with you personally *or* professionally. So you might find her asking your boss if a different colleague could work with her.

If you answered d), congratulations, this is assertive behaviour! This is the only response that enables you to find out the truth behind her intentions, and enables you to reply appropriately according to her response. If it was personal, she won't ask you again; if it was professional, she'll respect you for clarifying it and it'll prevent any awkwardness on either side moving forward.

Scenario 3: Your boss, who plays a significant role in your career progression, asks you to stay late again. This is the fourth Friday in a row, and you're frustrated that work is interfering with your personal life. How do you respond?

a). You agree to stay late, although you feel resentful.

b). You reluctantly agree but drag your feet.

c). You refuse.

d). You explain that while you're committed to your work, you also value your personal time.

Which option did you choose?

If you answered a), this is passive behaviour. The problem with this reaction is that your boss will not know that you were bothered by having to work late. They are likely to ask you again and again, thinking you're happy to stay. You might get the promotion you want but at what cost to your work/life balance? If you can't stand your ground at this level, what hope have you got at a higher grade?

If you answered b), this is passive-aggressive behaviour. The problem with this reaction is that your boss will know you're unhappy, but will not respect you or your attitude. They might ask you to stay late again to see if your attitude improves. If the same behaviour continues, you will not be promoted.

If you answered c), this is aggressive behaviour. The problem with this reaction is that, while you don't have to stay late, you will annoy your boss. They will not consider you a team player, and you are unlikely to be promoted.

If you answered d), congratulations, this is assertive behaviour! This is the only response that enables you to express your true feelings about staying late, and you offer a compromise without dumping a specific team member in it. While your boss might not like that you stood up to them, they will respect you. This is the only scenario where you are most likely to get what you want in the short-term (a night out with your friend) and in the long-term (a promotion).

If you've discovered that your predominant behaviour is passive, aggressive or passive-aggressive, it doesn't mean you're a bad person or you've done something wrong. These behaviours stem from System 1 because they're instinctive and cause you to *react* automatically: you do them without consciously thinking. They're habitual reactions to difficult situations that you'd rather not have to deal with. But why did we our reactive tendencies evolve in the first place?

5.04 Why Do People React Non-Assertively?

Our ability to be able to scan the environment for potential threats, and then react quickly, is a survival instinct that our ancient ancestors developed many years ago. They became so good at it that they could do it without conscious thought—that is, they could do it automatically and unconsciously, and with the minimum amount of effort or energy. This meant that they were able to rely on System 1 to alert them to the presence of a sabre-toothed tiger lurking in the undergrowth, for example, without specifically having to pay conscious attention to it. They could then devote System 2 to other pressing matters like searching for firewood.

If the threat is deemed real (actual or perceived), the stress response that immediately kicks into action is what is often referred to now as fight-flight-freeze: it describes the three different actions you might take. You might decide to fight the sabre-toothed tiger (aggressive behaviour), or you may flee from it as quickly as you can (passive behaviour). Alternatively, fighting and fleeing may not be a realistic option, perhaps in the face of bigger, faster predators, and so you may freeze: you may be immobilised to the point that you can't move or act—think rabbit in headlights—and hope the predator (or car!) won't spot you (passive behaviour).

When the stress response is triggered in your brain, it causes a rapid and complex chain of events: over thirty stress hormones are released, which cause around 1400 physiological and biochemical changes to occur within the body, all within seconds. As a result, your heart beats faster to increase oxygen and glucose supply to your major muscles, your blood thickens to enhance the availability of clotting agents and immune system cells in case of an injury, and your pupils dilate to heighten your vision. Your perception of pain is also diminished in readiness for an attack.[26]

If the part of our mind responsible for fight-flight-freeze was important for our ancestors, what about today? Although it still plays an important role in keeping us safe, times have changed. The dangers early humans faced were mostly physical threats to their lives (such as being eaten by sabre-toothed tigers). By contrast, the dangers many humans face today are mostly psychological, and stem from the pressures of modern life.

Even though modern-day threats seem as real to us as dangerous predators seemed to our ancestors, they are different: they're not actually life-threatening. Yet our reactions to them are the same. When someone or something causes you to feel a heightened emotion such as fear or anger, the fight-flight-freeze response kicks in and can cause you to irrationally overreact or underreact to the situation—reactions that you are most likely to regret either immediately or in the long term. Let's now consider some of the potential consequences of *reacting* in the workplace.

5.05 Non-Assertive Behaviour in Action

When people react aggressively at work, it can make the working environment highly uncomfortable. Sadly, it is not always easy to avoid this behaviour in the workplace because some organisations (or specific departments within organisations) reward aggressive behaviour. You'll often find that the staff in such organisations suffer silently with stress and panic attacks, burn out, or are plagued with addictions to external vices like gambling, drink, food and drugs. No doubt mental health problems in these organisations are prevalent (as is the frequency with which staff at such organisations resign from their roles).

What about reacting passively at work? While passive behaviour could be seen as effective in the workplace in lower grade roles

---

[26] West, M. (2021). *What is the fight, flight, or freeze response? Medical News Today.* https://www.medicalnewstoday.com/articles/fight-flight-or-freeze-response

(because junior staff are expected to do their job without dispute), staff displaying passive behaviour are not likely to be promoted to more senior roles because managers and leaders must be able to deal with difficult situations and conflict effectively.

At work, a person exhibiting passive behaviour might be taken advantage of because they never say 'no' or push back. This might leave them with a to-do list that they can't manage, which can be very stressful. They also might resent others around them because they've got less to do!

On a personal level, if passive behaviour results in you consistently holding back on how you *really* feel about someone or something you may find unexpressed anger, resentment and hurt building up—and all of these intense feelings eventually have to explode out somewhere. This explosion usually takes the form of an aggressive or emotional outburst at something trivial—one that may be directed at a loved one who has nothing to do with the original cause of resentment. Alternatively, you may withdraw into yourself, push down your emotions and use external vices such as junk food, alcohol, or nicotine to *keep* them pushed down.

In terms of reacting with passive-aggressive behaviour at work, the person does not express their true feelings and opinions (and so faces the same pent-up feelings and outbursts of anger, and the predisposition to external vices experienced by someone who exhibits passive behaviour). As a result, they don't get what they want (other than a twisted sense of satisfaction that stems from them punishing the person who upset them) and the other person loses out too.

This behaviour is likely to create a toxic environment of gossip and back-stabbing, and will probably mean that colleagues do not trust the person displaying passive-aggressive behaviour, making it highly likely that they will be avoided as much as possible.

Finally, the person who responds assertively at work ensures their professional relationships are healthy because they can express themselves to others in appropriate ways. This will leave their clients, colleagues and stakeholders feeling valued and respected. Their mental and emotional heath will be healthy and balanced too because they are not repressing negative emotions. Consequently, they are far less likely to feel the need to turn to external vices as outlined in Chapter 2.

If someone behaves assertively, they can actively influence their Success Cycle to turn in a positive way—one that helps them to achieve the results they want, without stepping on other people's toes to get there. While it can't guarantee that they will achieve the best outcomes for both them *and* the other party, it gives them their best shot. Of course, if they are expressing their thoughts and opinions openly and honestly, there is the chance that other people might not like them, but they will at least be respected! However, if someone doesn't like them because they are refusing to take on more than their fair share of work, for example, then would they want to be liked by them anyway?

Consider the chances of someone getting what they want when they react aggressively. While they might get what they want in the short-term, it's unlikely to endure in the long-term because other people will not cooperate with them. In fact, others might actively sabotage them (especially if they're passive-aggressive!).

What about reacting passively or passive-aggressively? These people are rarely going to get what they want simply because no one actually knows what it is they want!

As you can see, not only is responding assertively healthy for you and everyone else around you, but it also gives the Success Cycle the best chance of turning in a positive direction to get you what you want.

5.06 What Stops People Being Assertive?

Despite knowing that responding assertively is an adult behaviour, and that it represents your best shot at getting the success you want, an obvious question would be: why doesn't every adult respond in an assertive manner to every situation?

The simple answer is that assertiveness is a skill that has to be learnt: you need to know to use System 2 to interrupt System 1's default mode. If your parents reacted to situations in any way other than being assertive, it's likely that you followed their lead and found yourself reacting to similar situations in exactly the same way as them. It's highly unlikely that you or your parents received training in assertiveness at school, so it's difficult to break this cycle until this skill is more widely taught, either at school or in the workplace.

So, unless anyone has taught or shown you an alternative way, how are you supposed to fight against instinct and socialisation?

If you're not used to it, behaving in an assertive manner—especially when you're feeling a particularly negative emotion—can take self-discipline and courage no matter your previous automatic reactions: you need to make a concerted effort to engage System 2 to consciously choose your behaviour. In challenging circumstances, this could prove difficult—but it's not impossible. The next chapter reveals what you can do in these situations.

Now you know that you have a choice. And given that your life is unlikely to be under threat—especially at work—there's no reason for you only to be reactive in difficult situations. Remember, if you're reactive, System 1 is in the driving seat, which can make you feel like a victim of circumstance: out-of-control, and dis-empowered. (People often complain of being in 'fire-fighting' mode in a work context—a classic way of being that sits in the reacting camp.) On the other hand, if you are being *responsive*, System 2 is in the driving seat, which can make you feel empowered, in control, and on top of things.

Remember that this chapter is only looking at your behaviour, which isn't a direct reflection of who you *are*. It might echo how you feel on the inside or what you are thinking, but we'll look at the *cause* of your behaviour in Part Three.

Before you learn practical self-coaching strategies for engaging System 2 so you can over-ride System 1's autopilot and be assertive, let's answer a question I commonly get asked on my courses: Is assertiveness always the best option?

5.07 Is Assertiveness Always the Best Option?

You might expect my answer to this question to be 'you must always be assertive!' But that's not the case. It would be great if everyone could be assertive with everyone else all of the time—but we live in the real world, not an ideal one. So, in fact, my answer is: *choose* your behaviour by engaging System 2. This will enable you to *respond* consciously rather than *reacting* out of habit:

The next time you face a difficult situation (and you'll know it's difficult because it will cause you to feel a negative emotion such as anger, frustration, or stress), engage System 2 to make a conscious choice about the behaviour you think is most likely to get you what you want, without negatively impacting the other person. Then behave in that way. (There is a step-by-step guide on how to choose the best behaviour to get the best outcome in the next chapter.)

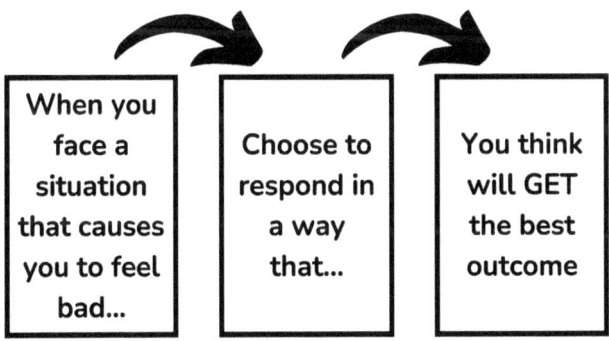

EXAMPLE: NEW JOB

Imagine that you've just started a new job and you're keen to prove your worth to your new boss. They ask you to do something that you think is beneath you. The best option if you're to get what you want (which, at the moment, is probably to prove your worth) is to suck it up and just do it! Yes, you're acting passively, but you are *choosing* to respond passively for a reason. Notice how different it feels to *choose* passive behaviour rather than just to react in that way because you think you have to, or because you don't have a choice.

EXAMPLE: HITTING A BRICK WALL

Now imagine that you've been on the phone to a call centre to resolve an issue with your phone. You have calmly and confidently described your problem but it's becoming clear that the person at the end of the line is not listening, and is not going to solve your problem anytime soon. In fact, you're sure they're trying to fob you off with a pre-prepared script! You've tried being assertive but you're not getting anywhere, so you choose to respond aggressively. Now they're listening to you! Notice how different it feels to *choose* this behaviour consciously rather than reacting in this way because you've lost your temper. Aristotle knew this:

"Anybody can become angry – that is easy. But to be angry with the right person and to the right degree and at the right time and for the right purpose, and in the right way – that is not within everybody's power and is not easy."

Before you learn *how* to respond in an assertive manner, you need to be clear about *who* and *what* currently cause you to react in a non-assertive manner. Let's do that now.

5.08 Who Are You Non-Assertive With?

The following activity will help you uncover the specific people and situations that trigger a reaction in you.

Activity 11: Honest Appraisal of Your Behaviour

As a result of the following activity, you might find that your behaviour depends on the person you are dealing with, or the situation in which you find yourself. You might be confident, articulate, and clear with some people, yet appear flustered, mumble your words and find your mind going blank when around others. You may also answer that you typically *react* one way at work and a different way at home.

Step 1 – Self-Reflection: Non-Assertive Behaviour At Work

Objective: Identify where assertive communication in the workplace could help you achieve your goals.

- Reflection:
  - Think about your behaviour at work when you feel stressed, nervous or uncomfortable. What specific people and/or situations cause you to behave non-assertively?
  - Consider how your behaviour impacts your Success Cycle. What insights does this give you? *For example, Sam realised that her avoidance tactics were increasing her stress levels and causing resentment toward her team, as she was working until 10 p.m. each night while they had lighter workloads.*
  - Revisit your professional goals from Chapter 2 and identify which goals could be achieved through being more assertive. *For example, Sam recognises that she needs to address Muhammed to ensure he follows through on her requests. She also knows she needs to speak with Belle about distributing work more fairly among her colleagues.*

Step 2 – Assessment of Non-Assertive Behaviour

Objective: Recognise patterns of behaviour that may prevent you from being assertive.

- Self-Assessment:
    - From what you learned in Step 1, consider the fears that may have contributed to your non-assertive behaviour. *For example, Sam says: "I avoid speaking to Muhammed and Belle for fear of confrontation. I am mainly concerned that they'd think I am not competent or capable."*
    - Can you detect any common theme to do with the people and situations that cause you to be non-assertive? For example, do you tend to be passive with more senior staff? Do you tend to be passive when you don't feel knowledgeable enough about a particular topic? *Sam realises that she is non-assertive with people who have more knowledge and experience than her.*
    - How has your non-assertive behaviour affected your relationships, reputation, and overall work performance?

Activity 11 - Sam's Insights:

"It's clear that my dominant behaviour at work is passive. Interestingly, I am not passive in my personal life; if anything, it would seem I'm aggressive. For example, if I'm particularly tired, or if I've had a really rough day at work and feel stressed (or more stressed than normal), I can be short and snappy with Davide over trivial things. I can explode at him for not putting his clothes in the washing basket, or for not putting the toilet seat down, or soaking the bathroom floor because he forgot to put a bath mat down (again). I get so angry that he ends up tip-toeing around me in case anything he does or says will set me off again.

Reading about the build-up of unexpressed anger being directed at a loved one really resonated with me. My aggressive outbursts towards Davide now make a lot of sense: it's because of my on-going passiveness at work.

In terms of passive-aggressive behaviour, I don't do this often but I can remember one occasion at work recently.

A few weeks ago, Belle asked me if I could stand in for her the following day to deliver a presentation to some stakeholders. I agreed to do it, of course, but I had already decided, in the back of my mind, that I would be phoning in sick the next morning so wouldn't have to do it. I resented the fact that she knows I hate doing last-minute presentations so giving me one night to learn fifty slides was inexcusable. What's more, the reason she gave me the last-minute task was due to a clash with a client brunch, which she could easily have rescheduled.

I knew I'd be landing her in it because she would have to do the presentation herself, but would only have about an hour to prepare for it. She would also have to let down her client at the last minute, which would have made her look bad. I was secretly glad!"

Chapter Summary

There are four types of behaviour—passive, passive-aggressive, aggressive and assertive—with the first three being *reactive* and reflexive in nature. When these behaviours occur automatically, System 1 is in control and defaults to its ancient fight-flight-freeze reaction. Assertiveness is the only *responsive* behaviour because it requires the intervention of System 2. This is why it needs to be learnt and practiced.

What's Next?

The next chapter shares a step-by-step strategy for choosing what you do when you are faced with threats, or difficult or uncomfortable situations. It shows you how you can engage System 2 to express yourself in a healthy way—one that ensures people like and trust you, that gets you what you want, and establishes healthy, balanced relationships too. Essentially, it shows you how to be more assertive, or choose the most appropriate behaviour that is most likely to get you the best outcome.

BUILDING ASSERTIVENESS: THE SKILLS YOU NEED

"When you choose the behaviour, you choose the consequences."
TobyMac[27]

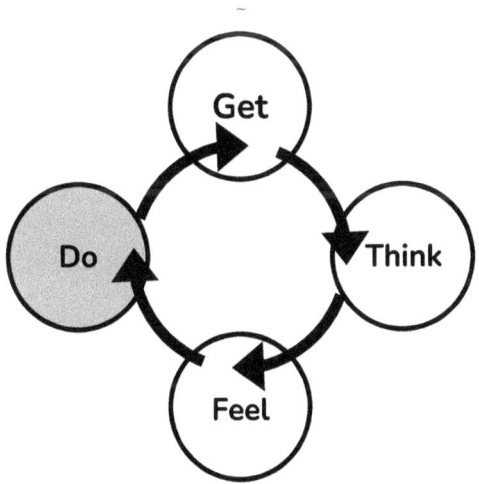

Sam is now consciously aware that her passive behaviour is at the heart of many of her problems at work because it causes her to accept more work without question, even when

---

[27] *TobyMac, whose real name is Toby McKeehan, is an American singer, rapper, songwriter, and record producer.*

she's already snowed under. Ultimately, by being passive, she is the one who loses out by working unsustainable hours and feeling stressed. It also causes her to feel increasingly frustrated each time she doesn't stand up for herself, or is defied by her colleague, or the distribution of work seems unfair.

Sam wants to engage System 2 to consciously change the direction of her Success Cycle so she can have a more manageable workload and can boost her chance of being promoted to Project Manager, all while feeling happier and calmer on the inside. It will also mean that she won't take her frustrations out on Davide when she gets home. To do this, she knows she wants to be more assertive at work, but she doesn't know how or where to start.

If you feel like Sam at the moment, fear not: this chapter teaches you how to be assertive in any situation. It shares a step-by-step process for choosing your behaviour, via System 2, which will give you the best chance of getting what you want while not negatively impacting others. It might feel uncomfortable and unnatural to begin with, but the more you practice the process, the easier it will become.

What This Chapter Covers:

- 6.01 Top Tips for Being More Assertive NOW
- 6.02 A Step-by-Step Approach to Being Assertive
- 6.03 How to Have an Assertive Conversation
- 6.04 Sam Confronts Belle and Muhammed
- 6.05 How to Decide in the Heat of the Moment

6.01 Top Tips for Being More Assertive NOW

Before you learn a step-by-step strategy to help you choose the best behaviour to get yourself the best outcome, here are some quick tips to help you change your behaviour consciously now.

If you would like to be less passive (and passive-aggressive) and more assertive, here's what you could practice doing:

- Notice if you say 'I don't mind', 'I don't know', or 'Don't worry about me' when someone asks what you want. Then practice saying what you *would* like. You could always start on the small stuff. For example, if someone asks, 'What would you like for dinner?' you can say, 'I'd like your delicious Moussaka, thank you.' When you're practiced at this you can move onto scenarios you find more difficult to offer your thoughts on.
- Practice giving your opinion. Again, start on the small stuff: say whether or not you liked a movie you saw and why, and then move onto the more important stuff.
- Practice using 'I' statements such as: 'I would like', 'I prefer', or 'I feel'.
- Take responsibility for the way you're feeling and act on it in an appropriate way rather than defaulting to a position that sees you taking revenge on the person that's caused you to feel that way.

If you would like to be less aggressive and more assertive, here are some tips for you:

- Practice letting others speak first. Even if you're desperate to share your thoughts or opinions, hold back on them until someone else has spoken up first.
- Become aware if you're interrupting someone. Stop yourself, apologise, and ask them to continue. Do not speak until they've finished.
- Practice asking what other people think. Make sure you give them your attention and listen to the answer.
- If you disagree with what someone else has said, avoid putting down the other person's point of view. For example, instead of saying: 'That's a stupid idea,' try something that

values their input: 'That's a really interesting idea. Shall I share my idea and then we can discuss the best way forward?'

These tips are incredibly useful because you can put them into practice straight away. Let's now delve into a somewhat more complex strategy to find out how you can engage System 2 to choose the most appropriate behaviour when you're faced with difficult situations, with the aim of achieving success.

6.02 A Step-by-Step Approach to Being Assertive

Here is a step-by-step strategy for helping you to choose your behaviour, which ensures you respond in the most fitting way to get you what you want:

1. Stop and take a breath
2. Release the emotion
3. Think about whether there is anything you can do about it
4. If YES, take action by considering the potential consequences and choosing the solution that is most likely to get you what you want
5. If NO, reframe it to feel better

Here's a visual representation of these steps:

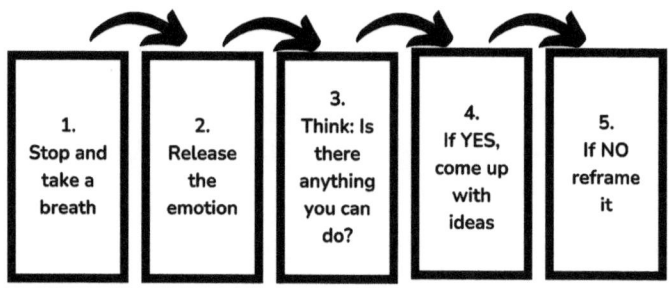

1. **Stop and take a breath.** This step interrupts System 1, preventing it from automatically defaulting to its 'fight-flight-freeze' instinct. It stops you from simply *reacting* and enables you to *respond* by engaging your neocortex.

   If you haven't got time to stop, then *react* in the best way you know how, but remember to come back to these steps afterwards so that you can learn from the situation. You can then go through the steps with the benefit of hindsight and think about what you *could* have done had you had time to think. In this way, you'll be mentally prepared to respond—rather than react—should you have to face a similar situation again.

2. **Release the emotion.** At some point in the process, give yourself permission to release the emotion in a way that's healthy and right for you. Some people need to talk it out; others need to physically let it out by exercising or punching a pillow or screaming at their bedroom wall; others need to cry. It's vital that you actively release the emotion at some point. If you don't, you could find yourself taking it out on a loved one instead. Just make sure you release the emotion in a way that doesn't negatively impact or harm another person.

   In some cases, you may find that you need to release the negative emotion before you are able to stop and take a breath. If so, that's absolutely fine, so long as you release it in a way that doesn't harm property or others.

3. **Think about whether there is anything that can be done about the situation** that's caused you to feel the negative emotion. This enables System 2 to step in and interrupt System 1's default mode.

4. **If the answer is yes, brainstorm all the possible solutions.** Then, decide which ones are feasible. Out of the feasible solutions, decide which ones you are prepared to adopt. Once you know this, consider the possible

consequences of your actions. Are they worth it? If yes, then you are going to have to use every ounce of your courage to speak up and take the necessary action. If not, then go to the next step.

5. **If the answer is no, then you can reframe it**—that is, find a way to think differently in order to feel better. We consider how to reframe a situation in Chapter 8.

Let's use one of Sam's scenarios to show you how this process works in practice. By way of some background information: Sam was promoted to a team leader position a couple of months ago. Muhammed is one of her team members who is almost twice her age and has been at the organisation for a lot longer than Sam, so is a lot more experienced. Although Muhammed was asked to apply for the team leader position—for reasons unknown to Sam—he didn't apply for it. Sam is struggling to manage Muhammed because he does his own thing, no matter what she asks him to do. Even when Sam specifically says 'Don't work on X project, work on Y project', Muhammed works on X project. Sam is at the end of her tether. To help her know what to do, Sam follows the step-by-step process. At Step 3, Sam knows there is something she can do and so she considers what her options are.

> ***Sam:*** *"One option is to continue to be passive by ignoring his behaviour. Another option is for me to be assertive and speak to him about his defiant behaviour. Or, I could be aggressive and go above his head and ask Belle to have a chat with him, and perhaps even move him to another team."*

The next step is to reflect upon the potential consequences of each option.

> ***Sam:*** *"If I continue to behave passively and ignore his behaviour, it could get worse. It could also undermine my authority with the other team members. By doing nothing, I'll also continue to feel frustrated every time I have to deal with him!*

If I behave assertively and speak to him, it could go one of two ways. It could clear the air and we could forge a healthy working relationship—but it could also make things worse because he might see our conversation as a confrontation and his behaviour might deteriorate as a result.

If I behave aggressively and go above his head without talking to him about it first, it could make things worse. He clearly doesn't respect me at the moment so imagine what he would think of me if I asked Belle to chat to him about an issue I'm having with him? And I would look incapable to Belle, which wouldn't be good— especially as she's already given me feedback that I need to be more authoritative with all of my team. Although if he were to move to another team, that would be good!"

Next, Sam considers which of these three options is most likely to get her what she wants without negatively impacting Muhammed.

Sam: *"Of course, being assertive is the grown-up, sensible thing to do, and is most likely to get the best outcome for both of us. If I'm assertive, he might even decide that moving to another team is best for him, which would be a result for me! As much as I would rather not have to speak to him, I know that I am going to have to force myself to do it, otherwise he will continue to annoy me."*

You can find out later what happens when Sam meets Muhammed to confront him about his defiance.

While assertiveness can't guarantee you will get what you want every time, it will give you the best shot, and having given it a go can make you feel good. Even if it doesn't work with some people or in some situations, it might work with others and in other situations.

Sometimes things happen that we can't change no matter how much we'd like to (i.e. bereavement, illness, pandemics, redundancy etc). While it's vital to deal at some point with the emotions these situations cause you, you must move forward or you risk being engulfed by emotion, which is likely to lead you into a state of anxiety, depression and/or an addiction to external vices. In these cases, one way to move forward—when you're ready—is to use 'reframing'. As highlighted already, the concept of reframing is covered in chapter 8, so I'll leave this for now, and will return to it later.

In the meantime, here's an activity to help you think about your behaviour and how you can engage System 2 to change it consciously.

 Activity 12: Habitual Behaviour

In Activity 11, you listed your typical types of behaviour, linked to your challenges at work. Pick one or two of the non-assertive behaviours you have been doing out of habit, and determine what you could do differently next time. You can use the following questions to help:

    a). Is there anything within your power that you could do about it?

    b). If yes, what can you do? What are the passive, assertive and aggressive options?

    c). What are the potential consequences of each option?

    d). Which of the options are likely to get you the best outcome (ones that won't harm anyone else in doing so)?

Activity 12 - Sam's Answer:

"I have a real-life situation I can use this method on straight away. Belle has asked me to deliver another presentation, but this time it's in about three hours, so I can't make up an excuse (or feign sickness!). But I feel terrified because I haven't got time to prepare properly. It's to our team. Is there anything I can do about it? Yes of course there is!

I could be passive, which would mean I'll have to do the presentation, which fills me with dread. I know I'll fluff it up and not only humiliate myself but my team will have even less faith in my capabilities, which is just going to make matters worse.

I could be assertive, which would mean being honest with her about how I feel and say that I really don't want to do it, but ask if there's someone else who could do it instead. Hopefully Belle would do it for me!

Or I could be aggressive, which would involve me telling her bluntly that I can't do it, but that's not going to bode well for my relationship with her nor my promotional ambitions.

It's obvious I need to choose assertiveness. I don't want her to think I'm not prepared to give it a go because it might affect how she views my promotion prospects. Equally, though, I can't keep making up little white lies or phoning in sick."

We'll find out shortly what happens when Sam has an assertive conversation with Belle. Before you do, it's useful to have a structure outlining how you can prepare for an assertive conversation.

6.03 How to Have an Assertive Conversation

Like any new behaviour, assertiveness is something you need to learn and practice if you're to be as effective as possible. Put another way: assertiveness is an adult, learnt behaviour, so you need to, well, learn how to do it. So how can you do this?

Your Perspective

Their Perspective

The best way to begin is to remind yourself that there are at least two people in any conversation, and so there are two perspectives:

Assertiveness is about sharing your thoughts and allowing the other person to share *their* thoughts before arriving at a compromise. So, you need to have a structure for your conversation to take this into account. Here's an outline of a conversation, which gives both parties an opportunity to speak:

1. Think through what specifically the issue is (from *your* perspective).
2. Explain the issue (as *you* see it) to the other person.
3. Ask for their response/explanation (as *they* see it from *their* perspective).
4. Listen carefully and don't interrupt, even if you disagree with them.
5. Say something to show you understand things from their perspective. Empathy is a good way to do this. This removes the possibility of them saying that you don't understand or you're not listening to them.
6. Say what you think or feel from *your* perspective. No one can dispute what you think or feel, but you must be honest about the real issue or you won't find a solution to fix the real issue.
7. Suggest what you want to happen or ask them what suggestions they have for moving forward. This is likely to require compromise from both side so you might not get exactly what you want but it's likely to be better than what you currently have got.

Here is a diagram if you prefer a visual representation of this process:

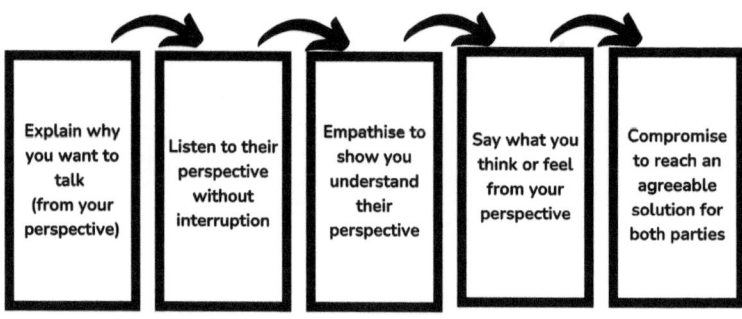

By using this process to consider your arguments and plan what you'd like to say you'll be better positioned to *respond* rather than *react*. Obviously, you can't predict what the other person is going to say, but at least you can be clear on what *you* want to say from *your* perspective. Practising can also calm your nerves if you're feeling a little jittery about the conversation.

6.04 Sam Confronts Belle and Muhammed

Let's find out how Sam gets on when being assertive with Belle.

Belle: *"I know it's last minute, but I want you to deliver this presentation to the team at 5pm today."*

Sam: *"I'm just so busy with my own workload at the moment, I don't think I've got time to give it justice and do a good job for you."*

Belle: *"Of your workload, what has to be done by end of play?"*

Sam: *"Just a few bits and pieces."*

Belle: *"Okay. So why don't you focus on finishing those few bits and pieces now and then start prepping for the presentation afterwards?"*

This can happen if you are not honest about the real reason you don't want to do something!

Sam: *"If I'm honest, I feel really ill-prepared to do it. I wouldn't mind doing it if I had lots of time to prepare for it, but just a couple of hours this afternoon isn't enough time for me. I feel sick thinking about it. Is there any way you could give it to someone else to do?"*

Belle: *"I could do it myself, but I know you want to progress in your career, and you deserve to progress. I can see huge potential in you, Sam, and as a Project Manager, you are going to have to do a lot of last-minute presentations. So, I want to give you an opportunity to practice in a low-risk environment. But it's up to you."*

Sam: *"Can I think about for a few minutes?"*

Sam had never considered that her manager was giving her a last-minute presentation to help her. She had assumed her manager was being lazy! However, she is left with a dilemma: on the one hand she is terrified of delivering a presentation with limited time to prepare; on the other, she really wants to be a Project Manager. Find out later what she decides to do.

Let's also find out how Sam gets on when she confronts Muhammed about his defiance:

Sam: *"I would like to talk to you about our working relationship. From my perspective, I get the sense that you don't respect me as your lead. I get this sense because you've ignored me on several occasions when I have asked you to do something, and have just done your own thing. And it feels to me like you're defying me. I'd love to hear your thoughts on this."*

Muhammed: *"I don't know what you mean! I do what you ask me to do, and I'm certainly not defying you!"*

Sometimes conversations can go this way when you first confront someone, so try again by giving specific examples.

Sam: *"Okay, so let me give you a couple of examples. Yesterday, I asked you to chase Painting Inc. for the documentation I needed to complete their file. However, I found out that you got Debs to do it. The day before, I asked you to send out an agenda for the team meeting but you didn't, so I had to do it at the last minute. On Monday, I asked you to finish the work you were doing on Organic Milk Ltd and get the file over to me before you left for the evening, but you left without doing what I'd asked. So, again, I had to complete it. This conversation is not so I can have a go at you. I'm trying to get to the bottom of what's going on so that we can work out a way of working together more productively."*

Muhammed: "If I'm honest, I don't think you're doing a very good job as team leader and think that I could do it better."

Sam: "Thank you for being honest with me, and I hear that you think you could do a better job as lead than me. Perhaps you're right, given your additional experience. From my perspective, I understand that you were asked to apply for the job as lead but you didn't, so I'm left feeling a little perplexed."

Muhammed: "You're right. I was asked but I was—and am—happy to stay at the level I'm at because I don't want the additional stress of extra responsibility for not much more money."

Sam: "I can understand that! So where does that leave us? I hear that you don't want the additional stress of extra responsibility, but you also don't want to listen to me as the person who is taking on the additional stress for not much more money."

Muhammed: "You're right. I know I've not been fair to you and I'm sorry. I get frustrated that there are better ways of doing some things and I don't like it when you ask me to do things that I don't think I should have to do. But I know that, unless I am prepared to take on the role of lead, there are things at my level that I just have to do even if I don't want to."

Sam: "Thank you for your apology. I appreciate it. I would love to hear your thoughts as and when you think you have a better way of doing things. I'd be more than willing to listen and do whatever is best for the business and clients. Equally, there are some tasks that I need you to do. I'd appreciate from now on if you could just do them. How does that sound?"

Muhammed: "That sounds fair."

Afterwards, Sam says:

"I'm buzzing! I'm blown away by how positive the conversation turned out. I just wish I'd done its weeks ago! I *feel like a huge weight has been lifted from my shoulders. Hopefully, Muhammed might have a bit more respect for me now, too."*

Once you've identified a situation, push yourself to have an assertive conversation. Use the ideas in this chapter to help you prepare, and then go for it! Of course, not every conversation will work out as successfully as these. Nonetheless, you might be surprised by what you learn from the other person's perspective.

Even if your assertive conversations don't go your way every time, at least you gave it your best shot. Notice how much more people will respect you for being honest about your needs while considering their needs too. If you choose to respond aggressively or passively, at least it's a choice—one that feels a lot more empowering than reacting out of habit or instinct.

You might find that some people get defensive when you behave assertively for the first time because they're so used to you being passive. This is perfectly normal: it might take some time for them to adjust to your newfound assertiveness skills. But do persevere. They'll get used to your new behaviour, and both of you can feel much happier before long.

On a slight tangent—but a highly relevant point nonetheless—think back to the Mehrabian Study highlighted in Chapter 4 where you won't be believed unless your verbal and non-verbal communication are congruent. This is key when practicing being assertive: you need to ensure your body language and voice match your words or you might find that you *still* don't get what you want.

So, when you practice being assertive, you must ensure your words and voice match your confident body language. If not, you risk not being believed and you will still be walked over. You could revisit Chapter 5 for some useful tips on how to look and sound confident.

A question I get asked a lot on my courses is: "What if I don't have time to think about how to respond?" Let's answer that question now.

6.05 How to Decide in the Heat of the Moment

Picture yourself in the following situation. You've had the morning from hell. Not only have you had an argument with your partner, but you've been lumbered with an additional load of work (again), which you don't have time to do, and the computer network is down. It just isn't your day. So, you might experience an 'amygdala hijack' [28]whereby your fight-flight-freeze response takes over: your emotions get the better of you and you react with an uncontrollable outburst.

Let's look at a couple of examples in which well-known people have over-reacted, only to regret it almost immediately.

EXAMPLE: THE MELTDOWN OF A MEDIA MOGUL

On 8 February 2011, acclaimed actor and television star Charlie Sheen gave an erratic and fiery radio interview. Frustrated by production delays due to his personal struggles, Sheen lashed out at the show's creator, Chuck Lorre, using derogatory and inflammatory language. The outburst ultimately led to his dismissal from the hit TV show *Two and a Half Men*, damaged his reputation, and became one of the most infamous Hollywood breakdowns in recent history.

EXAMPLE: A ROYAL RAGE

On 10 November 1992, during a visit to São Paulo, Brazil, King Charles III (then Prince Charles) was caught on camera losing his temper with a reporter. Frustrated by persistent media intrusion into his personal life— particularly his troubled marriage to Princess Diana— Charles muttered, unaware the microphone was still on, "Bloody people. I can't bear that man. I mean, he's so awful, he really is." The remark, broadcast to the world, exposed

---

[28] *In his book Emotional Intelligence, psychologist Daniel Goleman calls an overreaction to stress an 'amygdala hijack': the part of your brain responsible for keeping you safe (the amygdala) hijacks your response, and disables System 2's ability to intervene logically or rationally. As a result of this hijack, our response is unconscious: we react without really thinking.*

his frustration and resentment toward the press. Though minor compared to other public outbursts, this moment revealed a rare loss of composure from a royal figure who was expected to remain calm under pressure.

While your outbursts are unlikely to be as dramatic—or publicly announced around the world—they still happen. Here are some common examples of how an amygdala hijack might manifest in an office setting:

1. **The Door Slam Heard Around the Office**

   After receiving harsh criticism from their manager in a meeting, an employee storms out of the conference room and slams the door with such force that everyone in the office stops what they're doing. The awkward silence lingers, and the employee later regrets their reaction, realising they let their emotions take control.

2. **The Email You Shouldn't Have Sent**

   Feeling unfairly blamed for a project delay, an employee fires off a long, passive-aggressive email to their entire team, copying senior management. After hitting 'send', they immediately regret their tone, but the damage is done: relationships are strained, and they now have to do damage control.

3. **The Public Shouting Match**

   A usually calm supervisor loses their temper when an administrative assistant makes a small scheduling mistake. They raise their voice, berating the assistant in front of the entire office. The assistant, overwhelmed and embarrassed, bursts into tears. Later, HR gets involved, and the supervisor realises they've severely damaged their team's trust in them.

4. **The Rage Quit**

   After months of frustration and feeling unappreciated, an employee reaches their breaking point when their boss dismisses their concerns yet again. In a fit of anger, they blurt out, "I quit!" and walk out. Later, after cooling down, they realise they have no backup plan and wish they had handled things differently.

All of these examples illustrate people temporarily losing control due to stress, frustration, or anger—classic signs of an amygdala hijack. An *amygdala hijack* occurs when System 2 doesn't have a chance to intervene logically; it explains why not all behaviours can be changed using the power of System 2 alone. In Part 3, you will learn how to stop an amygdala hijack by reprogramming System 1.

In the meantime, a temporary loss of control doesn't mean you're powerless. Even if you've already reacted—slammed the door, sent the email, shouted at your assistant, or rage-quit—you can still learn from the experience. Once you've calmed down, remind yourself that you're human, which means you have a choice in how you respond, even after the damage has been done. You might choose to apologise to those affected, ask for your job back (if you want it), and—most importantly—forgive yourself for allowing an ancient fight-flight-freeze response to take over in the heat of the moment.

You can also reflect on how you might respond differently if a similar situation arises in the future. By doing so, you prepare yourself to make a different choice next time.

Here are some reflection questions to consider if you don't have time to respond in the moment:

- What was the outcome of your behaviour?
- Why did you react that way?
- Was it the best option?
- Did you make the right choice?
- If something similar happened again, what has this experience taught you about responding differently next time?

Before moving on to the next chapter, think about the specific steps you can take right now to harness the power of System 2 and be more assertive at work.

Activity 13: Action Plan

Apply the step-by-step process to have assertive communication in various work situations and reflect on the outcomes.

- Select 1–2 opportunities each day to practice assertiveness at work. Examples include:
- During a meeting, share your opinion or idea confidently.
- Address a task or request with clear boundaries (e.g., "I'm unable to take this on right now, but I can help next week.")
- After each interaction, take a moment to reflect on how it went:
- Did you use confident verbal and non-verbal behaviours (which you learnt in Chapter 3) to stay calm, composed, and assertive?
- Was your message communicated clearly and respectfully?
- How did others respond to your assertiveness?

Reflection:

- What challenges did you face while being assertive?
- What worked well, and what could you improve next time?
- How did practicing assertiveness affect your work performance and relationships?

By following this action plan, you will gradually build your assertiveness skills, enabling you to communicate more effectively, maintain healthier workplace relationships, and achieve your professional objectives. The key is to practice regularly, reflect on your experiences, and adjust as needed to continue growing your assertive communication skills.

Chapter Summary

It is possible to engage System 2 to *consciously* choose your behaviour by responding rather than letting System 1 run on default mode and reacting automatically. There is a step-by-step strategy that can help you plan and practice so you can get the best possible outcome. Your commitment to c*hoosing* your behaviour from now on is the first step in harnessing the power of System 2, learning to be more assertive, and turning the Success Cycle in a positive direction.

What's Next?

We've now finished our exploration of the do part of the Success Cycle. You now have strategies for consciously intervening so you can appear more confident and behave more assertively. It's now time to delve deeper into your **feelings**. Chapter 7 explores common fears in the workplace, revealing how feelings are linked to the way your mind interprets the world and how you experience reality. Chapter 8 shows that, because of the way that your mind works, it is possible to change how you feel in an instant so you can turn your fear into courage and help the Success Cycle flow in a direction that gets you what you want.

THE PSYCHOLOGY OF COURAGE: WHY WE HESITATE

"Fear defeats more people than any other thing in the world."
Ralph Waldo Emerson[29]

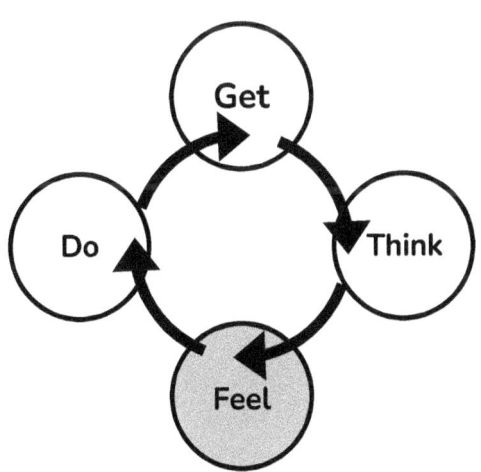

Belle asked Sam and her team to suggest ways to improve their service to stakeholders. Although Sam had an idea, she remained quiet, worried it might be dismissed as silly. She

---

[29] *Ralph Waldo Emerson (May 25, 1803 – April 27, 1882) was an American essayist, lecturer, philosopher, minister, and poet who played a leading role in the Transcendentalist movement of the mid-19th century. Known for championing individualism and critical thinking, he inspired generations with his writings and lectures.*

knows she needs to delegate more tasks to the team but fears it will cause conflict. At the same time, she recognises that delegation is crucial for her development: without freeing up time for complex tasks, she will struggle to advance in her career. However, her anxiety about unfamiliar tasks prevents her from delegating familiar ones, ultimately keeping her from tackling new challenges altogether. Sam recognises this as self-sabotaging behaviour and knows she must change, but she lacks the courage to take the first step.

Courage is fundamental to any leadership position, but fear can often hold people back. Like Sam, many professionals find themselves trapped in a cycle of hesitation, allowing fear to dictate their actions—or inaction. Understanding the nature of fear and how it shapes our decisions is the first step toward developing courage.

When we talk about fear at work, we're not referring to threats of physical harm (which are, hopefully, rare these days). Rather, we mean perceived psychological threats—those that influence our confidence, decision-making, and willingness to take risks.

This chapter explores what holds you back from being courageous at work and when it is wise to heed fear's warnings versus when it should be overridden. It delves into the root of fear, highlighting why an understanding of your mind is key to shifting your perspective. Ultimately, this chapter will show how your mind shapes your experience of the world—and what that means for boosting your courage at work.

What This Chapter Covers:

- 7.01 Assessing Your Courage
- 7.02 Emotions Versus Feelings
- 7.03 What Determines How You Feel?
- 7.04 What Lies at the Core of Courage?
- 7.05 How Meanings Shape Your Reality

7.01 Assessing Your Courage

Scott Steinberg, bestselling author of *Make Change Work for You*, outlines common types of fear that people report feeling in the workplace. We'll explore some of these in the following quiz, which can help you to discover if a lack of courage is causing your Success Cycle to flow in a way that leads to self-sabotage.

Listed below are questions about six of the most common fears. Your job is to read the possible answers ('Yes', 'Sometimes', and 'No') and decide which one best describes you in each case.

1. **Do you fear public speaking?**

   - **Yes.** You avoid it at all costs because the thought of being the centre of attention with all eyes on you and your credibility on the line fills you with dread.

   - **Sometimes.** You don't mind it as long as you know the topic well or the audience knows less than you.

   - **No.** You might get nervous for the first few minutes, but then you feel alive. Presentations are an opportunity to share your thoughts and ideas with a captive audience!

2. **Do you fear failure?**

   - **Yes.** You worry about failure so much that you don't try something new, focussing on the fact that you might fail.

   - **Sometimes.** You'll give it a go if you have someone who believes in you or supports you fully. Otherwise, you won't.

   - **No.** You don't believe in failure. You would rather regret trying something than regret not trying it. In the words of Susan Jeffers: "Feel the fear and do it anyway."

3. **Do you fear change?**

   - **Yes.** You fret about any changes around you, whether in people or the situation. You worry so much that, at the merest hint of change, you do your best to resist or prevent it.

- **Sometimes.** You worry when things change and prefer stability. But after the initial wobble, you accept that things will work out in the end and don't resist too much.
- **No.** You think life is boring without change, so you embrace it. After all, 'change is the only constant!'

4. **Do you fear not being good enough?**
   - **Yes.** You worry constantly that you won't measure up against your peers or that you won't be able to complete the task at hand.
   - **Sometimes.** You don't compare yourself to others when you know you're good at something, but when you're unsure of your abilities, you doubt yourself and worry that you aren't good enough.
   - **No.** You understand that it's impossible to be good at everything. You accept your strengths and work on areas you want to improve.

5. **Do you fear not being liked?**
   - **Yes.** You worry that if you say 'no', confront someone, or speak your mind, people might not like you. As a result, you say 'yes', avoid confrontation, and stay quiet when asked for your opinion.
   - **Sometimes.** You don't care if some people like you, but there are others who matter more to you, and you become a people-pleaser.
   - **No.** You know it's impossible to be liked by everyone. It's important to you to treat others how you would like to be treated yourself, but whether they like you or not is their choice.

6. **Do you fear losing control?**
   - **Yes.** You like to have a tight grip on what you're doing and worry that, if you let go just a little, it'll all come crumbling down. As a result, you find delegating incredibly difficult.

- **Sometimes.** You're fine letting your partner take control in your personal life, but you fear losing control in your professional life (or vice versa).
- **No.** You know that control is just an illusion, so you have no problem letting go.

If you answered 'no' to all the questions, congratulations—you are already courageous! However, if you mostly chose 'yes' or 'sometimes', fear may be driving your Success Cycle in a negative direction. But don't worry: you'll learn in Chapter 8 how to change how you feel so you can be more courageous.

To do this, you first need to understand the difference between emotions and feelings—and how they relate to courage.

7.02 Emotions Versus Feelings

While many people often use the words 'emotions' and 'feelings' interchangeably, they are actually different. At a technical level, not everyone agrees on where emotions come from or what constitutes an emotion. However, for simplicity, I've chosen to use the most common views, which are also the easiest to understand.

In a 2010 *Scientific American* article, Ferris Jabr discusses Charles Darwin's 1872 publication *The Expression of the Emotions in Man and Animals*. Jabr notes that Darwin argued 'all humans, and even other animals, show emotion through remarkably similar behaviours.' He goes on to say, 'For Darwin, emotion had an evolutionary history that could be traced across cultures and species—an unpopular view at the time. Today, many psychologists agree that our basic emotions are developed through evolution and are universal to all humans, regardless of culture.' [30]

Arguably the most well-known and influential of these psychologists is Paul Ekman, who inspired the hit TV series *Lie to*

---

[30] Jabr, F. (2010). The Evolution of Emotions: Charles Darwin's little-known psychology experiment. Scientific American. https://blogs.scientificamerican.com/observations/the-evolution-of-emotion-charles-darwins-little-known-psychology-experiment

Me. In the 1960s, Ekman identified six basic emotions: anger, fear, surprise, disgust, happiness, and sadness. He expanded this list in the 1990s to include contempt, amusement, contentment, embarrassment, excitement, guilt, pride in achievement, relief, satisfaction, sensory pleasure, and shame.[31]

In short, it is commonly believed that emotions are the result of an external stimulus triggering physical sensations in the body to help ensure human survival (i.e., 'fight-flight-freeze'). For example, imagine you are alone in a dark alley late at night, and you see a large silhouette of what appears to be a person running toward you. You instantly feel fear, your heart pumps faster, your breathing speeds up, and your stomach tightens as your body prepares either to run or to fight. This is considered a 'normal' human reaction to an external stimulus that is perceived as a threat. The physical sensations caused by the stimulus will subside once the threat is over, and you will no longer feel fear.

While emotions are in the realm of the body, feelings exist in the realm of the mind: they are shaped by individual experiences and reflect what happens in your mind when you experience emotions. For example, imagine being back in that dark alley. The large silhouette of a person runs toward you, triggering the emotion of fear. However, the figure runs straight past you towards a bus stop at the end of the alley, which he reaches just as a night bus screeches to a halt. The feelings you experience after this could vary from person to person. Some might feel relief, others might feel relaxed, while others might feel invigorated. In this case, the emotion of fear comes first, and it is universal; the subsequent feelings, however, vary depending on the individual and the situation.

Understanding the difference between emotions and feelings is crucial for distinguishing between 'normal' fear and fear that arises from other sources. Let's explore the Ninety Second Rule to clarify this further.

---

[31] *For more information on Paul Ekman and his findings, visit https://www.paulekman.com*

The Ninety Second Rule

The idea that emotions are usually temporary, but that the feelings they provoke can endure and accumulate over time, is supported by Jill Bolte-Taylor, a neuroanatomist and author of *My Stroke of Insight*. She explains:

> "When a person has a reaction to something in their environment, there's a ninety second chemical process that happens in the body. After that, any remaining emotional response is just the person choosing to stay in that emotional loop. Something happens in the external world and chemicals wash through your body, which puts it on full alert. It then takes less than ninety seconds for those chemicals to totally flush out of your body. This means that, for ninety seconds, you can watch the process happening, you can feel it happening, and then you can watch it go away. After that, if you continue to feel fear, anger, and so on, you need to look at the thoughts that you're thinking that are re-stimulating the circuitry that is resulting in you having this physiological response over and over again."

In short, Bolte-Taylor is saying that when you feel an emotion in response to a certain event or stimulus—and that response is justified and 'normal,' lasting less than ninety seconds—you are simply experiencing your body's natural 'fight-flight-freeze' response. This is an example of 'normal' fear, to which you should pay attention and take appropriate action. However, if the feelings persist beyond ninety seconds, they are being driven by something else.

EXAMPLE: SAM'S PRESENTATION NERVES

In Chapter 2, Activity 1a, Sam described a situation in which she had to deliver a presentation to ten important stakeholders. She had enough time to feel fully prepared, so when she stood up to begin, adrenaline coursed through her body: her heart beat faster, her blood pressure surged, and her breathing increased rapidly. She felt afraid as she scanned the expectant faces in the audience. However, after delivering the first couple of sentences, she realised that there was no threat to her safety because she was fully prepared. As a result, her body stopped producing the hormones that had been stimulating her adrenal glands to release adrenaline, and she calmed down.

If Sam had continued to feel fear for longer than ninety seconds, however, Bolte-Taylor's theory suggests that her thoughts would have taken over, prolonging her state of fear. For instance, if she hadn't felt prepared, she might have thought that the stakeholders were judging her, feared forgetting her words, or worried about looking silly and harming her career. In this case, her thoughts and feelings would have re-stimulated the fear circuitry, rather than the actual experience of giving the presentation itself.

To reiterate, feelings of fear that last longer than ninety seconds indicate that they have been triggered by something other than the automatic fight-flight-freeze response. This type of fear can hinder your courage and hold you back at work—but it is also the kind of fear that can be overridden using System 2.

But how and why do your fears last for more than 90 seconds? To answer this, let's revisit the NLP Communication model you first encountered in Chapter 3.

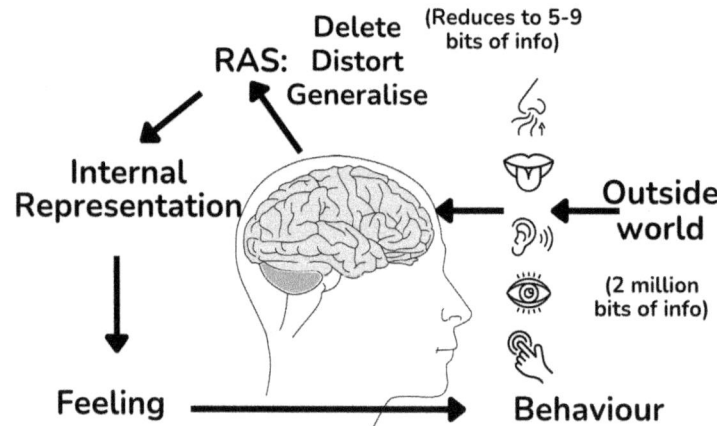

7.03 What Determines How You Feel?

In Chapter 3, you learned that your brain has a powerful filtering system—the Reticular Activating System—which helps you to cope with the stimulus-rich environments in which you live. To recap: your brain processes around 2 million bits of information from the world around you at any given time. However, it can only consciously process 5 to 9 chunks. To manage this, your brain uses deletion, distortion, and generalisation to filter out what's unnecessary and highlight what's important. This helps you focus on the relevant information in real time.

But there's more. To add another layer of complexity, your brain doesn't just filter information; it also interprets it and assigns meaning. This is where the magic happens. Your brain creates an internal representation—or model—of the external world. This internal model influences how you feel—whether positively, negatively, or neutrally. And your feelings, in turn, directly affect your behaviour and, ultimately, the outcomes you get.

Let's consider a simple example. Imagine you're in the office, fully absorbed in your work. Suddenly, you smell smoke, hear an unusual crackling sound, and see your colleagues glancing around, clearly noticing the same things. You then hear the blaring siren of a fire alarm. Your brain filters the external information, ignoring things like email notifications or phone calls. At that moment, your brain draws from its database of past experiences, knowledge, and learned information, concluding that the building is on fire. This interpretation triggers the acute stress response, putting your body into fight or flight mode, and you feel fear and urgency, pushing you to escape quickly. In this case, System 1 has done its job: it's kept you safe.

This example illustrates how attributing meaning to external events is essential for survival. By assigning meaning, your brain prepares you to respond appropriately to what's happening around you. Because this process occurs automatically, outside of your conscious awareness, it is an example of System 1 at work.

7.04 What Lies at the Core of Courage?

But what is the 'internal representation' or 'internal model', and how does it influence the Success Cycle? To answer these questions, let's explore the concept of 'maps' and three key presuppositions on which the NLP Communication Model depends:

People Create Maps	The Map Is Not The Territory	People Respond To Their Map of Reality, Not To Reality

'People Create Maps'

When you store information as an internal representation, you create a 'map' in your mind that represents your interpretation of an external event. In other words, everyone creates their own internal model or 'map' of reality: your map is your perception of reality.

'The Map is Not The Territory'

This phrase was coined by Polish-American scholar Alfred Korzybski. It reflects the fact that a whole reality exists outside of your mind, but you can only construct partial models of this 'territory' based on the information you've gained through your senses. Therefore, your 'map' is not a true representation of an external event (or territory): it's your version, or interpretation, of it. You wouldn't confuse a road map with a road, or a menu with a meal, so why would you confuse your interpretation of reality with reality? [32]

---

[32] This is based on Alfred Korzybski's 1933 seminal work, Science and Sanity: An Introduction to Non-Aristotelian Systems and General Semantics.

'People Respond to their Map of Reality, not to Reality'

When things happen in the external world, you respond to your 'map' of these events, not to the entirety of reality. Think of it as the difference between objective reality and subjective interpretation: all of reality is objective reality; your map of reality is a subjective interpretation of it. Let's explore this difference in a bit more detail.

Look at the picture of the cat below. The objective reality is that the cat is a cat, but the cat's subjective interpretation is that it is a tiger (assuming cats have subjective interpretations, of course!)

EXAMPLE: FELINE FUR

Imagine you're eating lunch in a café you regularly visit. You're enjoying your favourite menu choice when you feel fur rubbing against your leg and hear a rhythmic purring sound, along with the jingling of a tiny bell. (Your senses are feeding information to your brain.) Your brain associates that feeling and the sounds with the fluffy four-legged animal you see at your feet and groups the experience under the heading of 'cat'. (Your brain is generalising the sensory information based on previous experiences of feeling similar sensations and hearing similar sounds.)

The cat rubbing against your leg is the objective reality. However, 'cat' in itself has no inherent meaning. Your brain must interpret what 'cat' means to you. It refers to its database of previous experiences with 'cats' to determine your emotional response and behaviour. So, if you love cats, you'll feel happy and will bend down to give it a cuddle. If you dislike cats, you'll feel irritated and shoo it away with your foot. If you neither like nor dislike cats, you'll likely feel indifferent and ignore it.

Every time something happens in your life, your brain follows the same process: it compares what your senses perceive with past experiences to generate a response. In essence, you are reading your personal map of reality.

While an objective reality exists—giving presentations, going into lockdown, getting a new job, being made redundant, retiring, etc.—events themselves have no inherent meaning. Instead, you assign meaning based on how your brain interprets what's happening, shaping your subjective 'map' of reality. It's a bit like wearing virtual reality glasses.

In this way, it's your 'map'—not the events themselves—that influences how you feel about life's experiences. Your 'map' drives your automatic reactions and behaviours, often beyond your conscious awareness.

You can think of your brain as operating in a similar way to a lawyer. A defence attorney presents evidence to a jury in a way that frames their client as innocent, while a prosecutor presents the same evidence in a way that frames the same person as guilty. The 'winner' is usually the one who is best able to convince the jury of their version of reality—the one who can convey their map of reality most compellingly—rather than who is objectively right or wrong. Both you and I are doing this every moment of every day: we're framing our experiences of reality to fit our preconceptions.

Let's explore in more detail how the meanings you assign to external events shape your reality, and how they can set the Success Cycle in motion—either in a positive or negative direction.

7.05 How Meanings Shape Your Reality

When you attach a positive meaning to an event, you generate emotions and behaviours that reinforce success. Conversely, if you assign a negative meaning, it can create a self-fulfilling cycle that leads to failure or stagnation. Since events themselves have no inherent meaning, your brain interprets them based on your past experiences, ideas, thoughts and emotions. These interpretations form your internal model of reality, which in turn drives your responses. You don't react directly to the external world—you react to your perception of it. Let's take a look at a couple of examples.

EXAMPLE: THE STUDENT AND THE EXAM

A university student sits down for an important exam. As she reads the first question, she realises it covers a topic she found difficult during revision. Instead of seeing this as a disaster, she interprets it as a challenge she can work through. She assigns it the meaning of an opportunity to apply what she knows, and this interpretation allows her to stay calm and focused, helping her think clearly and recall information effectively. As a result, she performs well and earns a high grade.

Meanwhile, another student sees the same question and immediately interprets it as confirmation that the exam is too difficult. He assigns the experience the meaning of inevitable failure, which causes him to feel frustrated and anxious. His concentration falters, leading to rushed answers and mistakes. As a result, he performs poorly and receives a lower score.

The exam itself wasn't the cause of either student's success or failure. It was their *interpretation* of the situation and the meaning they attached to it that shaped their responses and ultimate outcomes.

EXAMPLE: THE ENTREPRENEUR AND THE BUSINESS SETBACK

An entrepreneur launches a new business, but in the first few months, sales are slow. He interprets this as a normal phase for any startup and assigns it the meaning of a learning curve. Because of this, he remains proactive—adjusting his marketing, seeking advice, and refining his approach. Over time, his persistence leads to growth and success.

In contrast, another entrepreneur experiences the same slow start but interprets it as evidence that the business will never work. She assigns it the meaning of personal failure. Discouraged, she hesitates to invest more time and effort, and eventually, she gives up.

In both cases, the external situation was the same. What shaped their outcomes was not the event itself, but how they interpreted it and the meaning they assigned to it.

In essence, System 1 operates in default mode, relying on your 'map' or internal model to interpret and make sense of what is happening in and around you. It does this outside of your conscious awareness, allowing you to focus on more pressing tasks, such as planning next year's projections or preparing the agenda for a team meeting.

Since there is little in the way of absolute truth, we accept as true only what we convince ourselves to be true. And because we like to be right, we shape our interpretation of events to align with our existing worldview. This, in turn, sets off the Success Cycle in either a positive or negative direction, depending on whether the assigned meaning is constructive or limiting.

Let's look at another example. This time, a company announces an internal restructuring, which includes changes to reporting lines and job responsibilities.

Person 1: The Optimist

Interpretation: *"This is an exciting opportunity to develop new skills and grow within the company."* Behaviour: They proactively seek out information about the changes, engage with leadership to understand how they can contribute, and look for ways to leverage the restructuring for career advancement.

Likely Outcome: Their positive mindset fuels a Success Cycle that opens doors for growth, strengthens relationships with leadership, and increases their chances of securing a more fulfilling role.

Person 2: The Sceptic

Interpretation: *"This might lead to job insecurity or added pressure without additional compensation."*

Behaviour: They take a wait-and-see approach, avoid openly expressing opinions, and focus on maintaining job performance while quietly exploring external job opportunities as a backup plan.

Likely Outcome: Their cautious approach keeps them prepared, but their reluctance to engage may limit their opportunities for advancement within the company, potentially stalling their Success Cycle.

Person 3: The Pessimist

Interpretation: *"This is a sign that the company is struggling, and my role might be at risk."*

Behaviour: They disengage, resist change, and vent frustrations to colleagues, which may lower team morale. They might also start looking for a new job immediately out of fear rather than assessing the situation rationally.

Likely Outcome: Their negative outlook triggers a negative Success Cycle, increasing stress, reducing their job satisfaction, and potentially leading them to make impulsive career decisions that limit their long-term opportunities.

Although the restructuring itself is neutral, each individual's internal 'map' of reality shapes their perception and response. Their mind dictates whether they see the change as an opportunity, a risk, or a threat—ultimately influencing their behaviour, career trajectory, and overall success.

The good news is that your internal model of reality is flexible: it is possible to engage System 2 to consciously change your interpretations and create a more empowering Success Cycle. Before learning how to do this, let's explore the meanings you currently assign to external events that may be causing your Success Cycle to flow in a negative direction. To do this, you will need the table you created in Activity 3 in Chapter 2, where you visually mapped the relationship between your objectives and self-sabotaging behaviours.

Activity 14 - The Meanings You Assign

Step 1: Revisit Your Objectives

- Revisit your objectives and their corresponding self-sabotaging behaviours, which you identified in Activity 3, Chapter 2.

- Example: *I want to be able to give feedback, but I tend to keep quiet.*

Step 2: Identify the Emotional Impact

- How do you feel when you engage in self-sabotaging behaviour?

- Example: *When I don't give feedback, I feel frustrated.*

Step 3: Understand the Meaning You Assign

- What do you think this behaviour says about you or the situation?

- Example: *If I were to give feedback, I might upset the other person.*

Step 4: Identify Common Themes

- What common themes do you notice?

Activity 14 - Sam's Answer:

1. Getting Muhammed to do what I ask

- **Self-Sabotaging Behaviour:** Avoid speaking to him about his behaviour.
- **How I Feel:** Fine, because I've already had an assertive conversation with him.
- **What It Means to Me:** I believe the issue has been addressed, so I don't need to bring it up again.

2. Speaking up and sharing my ideas in meetings

- **Self-Sabotaging Behaviour:** I keep quiet.
- **How I Feel:** Angry and frustrated.
- **What It Means to Me:** I worry that I might say something silly.

3. Shouting about my strengths

- **Self-Sabotaging Behaviour:** I downplay my abilities.
- **How I Feel:** Uncomfortable.
- **What It Means to Me:** If people expect too much from me, I might disappoint them.

4. Speaking to Belle about my colleagues not doing their fair share

- **Self-Sabotaging Behaviour:** I avoid speaking to Belle and do the extra work myself.
- **How I Feel:** Fine, because I've had an assertive conversation with her.
- **What It Means to Me:** I've already taken action, so I don't need to dwell on it.

5. Doing new tasks outside my comfort zone

- **Self-Sabotaging Behaviour:** I avoid new tasks.

- **How I Feel:** Stressed.
- **What It Means to Me:** If I fail, people will think I'm an imposter.

6. Delivering last-minute presentations

- **Self-Sabotaging Behaviour:** I make excuses to avoid them.
- **How I Feel:** Terrified.
- **What It Means to Me:** If I don't prepare enough, I might say something wrong, and people will think I'm not capable.

7. Switching off from work

- **Self-Sabotaging Behaviour:** I work in the middle of the night.
- **How I Feel:** Exhausted.
- **What It Means to Me:** If I don't stay on top of everything, people will think I'm not capable.

8. Letting go and moving on when things don't go well

- **Self-Sabotaging Behaviour:** I focus on what I did wrong.
- **How I Feel:** Stressed.
- **What It Means to Me:** If I made a mistake, it means I'm not good enough.

Sam's Common Themes:

"The common theme seems to be that I worry about being found out as incapable, an imposter, or not good enough. This would explain why I don't like celebrating my successes: if I put myself down first or downplay my abilities, I can't be exposed. It also explains why I dread presentations for which I can't prepare adequately: my lack of preparation would

reveal my lack of knowledge and capability, especially if people ask me questions I can't answer.

It also explains why I don't like saying 'no' to more senior members of staff: I'm afraid they'll think I'm not capable of doing the job and that I'll be fired. This fear also drives me to over-prepare: I'm constantly trying to stay on top of my work so that I can't be exposed as incapable or as an imposter."

Chapter Summary

Emotions and feelings shape your actions and reactions, influencing the Success Cycle. Emotions are universal and triggered by external stimuli (often tied to survival instincts), while feelings are shaped by our individual experiences and perceptions. Emotions are brief, physical reactions that arise in response to external events, whereas feelings are the mental interpretations of those emotions.

People create mental maps based on their past experiences, beliefs, and emotions. These maps influence how you interpret external events and drive your behaviour. The key presuppositions of NLP (Neuro-Linguistic Programming) emphasise that your internal map is not an accurate reflection of reality, but rather a subjective interpretation. As a result, the meaning you assign to external events—whether positive or negative—shapes how you feel (fearful or courageous), which in turn impacts the flow of the Success Cycle and the outcomes you achieve.

Since meanings are subjective, not objective, it is possible to harness the power of System 2 to change them.

What's Next?

Now that you understand the meanings you assign to people and situations that cause you to feel fearful, next you'll learn how to override System 1's default mode. By doing so, you can change the meaning of the things that may currently trigger negative feelings, helping you feel more courageous and ensuring your Success Cycle flows in a positive direction, leading to more positive outcomes for you.

8

CULTIVATING COURAGE:
THE SKILLS TO FACE FEAR HEAD-ON

"Courage is resistance to fear, mastery of fear
—not absence of fear."
Mark Twain[33]

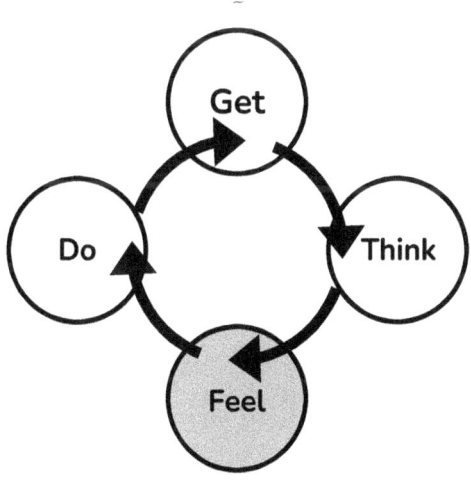

Sam initially assumed that Belle had asked her to do a last-minute presentation because she was too lazy to do it herself.

---

[33] *Samuel Langhorne Clemens (November 30, 1835 – April 21, 1910), better known as Mark Twain, was an American writer, humourist, and essayist. Hailed by William Faulkner as "the father of American literature," Twain's most famous works include The Adventures of Tom Sawyer (1876) and its sequel, Adventures of Huckleberry Finn (1884).*

This assumption led to resentment, which would typically trigger passive or passive-aggressive behaviour. However, when Sam discovered the real reason—Belle wanted to give her an opportunity to gain experience and fast-track her path to becoming a Project Manager—her perspective shifted instantly. Resentment was replaced with admiration and respect. As a result, she felt more courageous and was able to assert herself with Belle effortlessly.

Sam's experience highlights how quickly feelings can change when we change the meaning behind an event. For Sam, this shift happened naturally, but it's also possible to engage System 2 to make these changes consciously.

Courage isn't an inherent trait—it's a skill shaped by the interpretations System 1 assigns to external events. These interpretations influence how the Success Cycle unfolds, shaping self-fulfilling patterns that define your reality.

This chapter guides you through techniques that interrupt this cycle by activating System 2 to reassess the meanings you attach to events, reshape your responses, and create better outcomes. By doing so, you can turn hesitation into opportunity—transforming fear into a catalyst for courage, confidence, and progress.

What This Chapter Covers:

- 8.01 Quick Fixes to Feel More Courageous
- 8.02 A Technique for Feeling Courageous
- 8.03 Reframing: A Step-By-Step Process
- 8.04 Reframing: Practice with General Examples
- 8.05 Reframing: Practice with Your Own Objectives

8.01 Quick Fixes To Feel More Courageous

Before diving into a deeper, longer-lasting, but more complex technique to change how you feel, let's explore some quick and simple ways to change how you feel in order to boost your courage.

Mind Your Language

The old saying *"sticks and stones may break my bones, but words will never hurt me"* isn't entirely true. Words have immense power over how you feel. In the context of the Success Cycle, your feelings drive your behaviour, which then determines your outcomes.

Think about the words *hate, battle, despise, warpath,* and *confrontation.* How do they make you feel? Now consider *calm, happy, lucky, content,* and *positive.* Notice the difference?

According to Andrew Newberg, M.D. and Mark Robert Waldman in their book *Words Can Change Your Brain*, a single word can influence the switching on of genes that regulate physical and emotional stress. Positive words activate the brain's motivational centres, while negative words stimulate the amygdala (the brain's fear centre), triggering stress hormones that impair logic, reason, and communication.

So, who controls the words you use?

The answer is you. One of the simplest ways to shift how you feel is to mind your language. Look at the following examples and notice how changing the words alters the emotional impact:

- Presentation → *Chat*
- Networking → *Work party*
- Confrontation → *Addressing an issue*
- Issue → *Topic*
- Conflict → *Difference of opinion*

Do the words on the right feel less intimidating? This simple technique—reframing the language you use—can make a significant difference to how you perceive and react to events.

So, the next time someone asks you to give a presentation (which might make you feel nervous), think of it as simply having a chat with a group of people (which feels less daunting). If you're invited to a networking event and don't enjoy them, imagine it's just a work party—a casual gathering with colleagues.

By changing your words, you change your perspective.

Laughter: The Best Medicine

In addition to feeling good, laughter can induce physical changes in your body. When you start laughing, you take in oxygen-rich air, which stimulates your heart, lungs and muscles, as well as increasing the endorphins that are released by your brain. Once you've stopped, it cools down your stress response by decreasing your heart rate and blood pressure. The result? A good, relaxed feeling. Laughter can also stimulate your circulation and aid muscle relaxation, both of which can help reduce some of the physical symptoms of stress.[34]

According to Dr. Gulshan Sethi, the head of cardiothoracic surgery at the Tucson Medical Centre and faculty at the University of Arizona's Centre for Integrative Medicine:[35]

> "Laughter activates the body's natural relaxation response. It's like internal jogging, providing a good massage to all internal organs while also toning abdominal muscles."

So why not watch a show of your favourite comedian, or hang out with a friend who makes you laugh?

---

[34] Mayo Clinic Staff. *Stress relief from laughter. It's no joke.* 5 April 2019. Mayo Clinic. www.mayoclinic.org/healthy-lifestyle/stress-management/in-depth/stress-relief/art-20044456

[35] Tamara Lechner. *6 Reasons Why Laughter is the Best Medicine.* 11 Sept 2015. Chopra. www.chopra.com/articles/6-reasons-why-laughter-is-the-best-medicine

Move to Improve Your Mood

Physical activity has a positive impact on mood, according to studies carried out by Martina Kanning and Wolfgang Schlicht from the University of Stuttgart. They asked participants to rate their mood immediately after periods of physical activity (after going for a walk or doing housework, for example), and periods of inactivity (after reading a book or watching television, for example). The researchers found that the participants felt more content, more awake, and calmer after being physically active compared to after periods of inactivity. They also found that the effect of physical activity on mood was greatest when mood was initially low.[36]

So what are you waiting for? The next time you're feeling a little low, do an activity that makes your heart beat faster. What you choose is up to you. You can do whatever you enjoy and is easily accessible: you could go for a walk, jog or run, pump iron at the gym, take your bike for a spin, jump on a trampoline, dance the night away, or swim a few lengths.

Music Be The Food of Love

Music has been part of human culture for thousands of years and has been proven to be so powerful that it can help rewire damaged parts of the brain. This can be seen in the film *Alive Inside: A Story of Music and Memory*, which shows how Dan Cohen, a social worker, uses music to unlock memory in nursing home patients. It shares examples of people who seem lost in their own minds but become animated after a few minutes of listening to familiar music.

Why don't you tap into this ancient stimulus and listen to music that uplifts you?

According to the Examined Existence website, "soothing tunes foster the release of serotonin, a hormone that fosters happiness and a general sense of well-being. It also flushes the body with dopamine,

---

[36] Martina Kanning. *Using Objective, Real-Time Measures to Investigate the Effect of Actual Physical Activity on Affective States in Everyday Life Differentiating the Contexts of Working and Leisure Time in a Sample with Students*. 1 Jan 2012. Frontiers in Psychology. www.researchgate.net/publication/235368609

a neurotransmitter that makes you feel good. Music also paves the way for the release of norepinephrine, a hormone that brings about euphoria and elation."[37]

So select your favourite, mood-enhancing tune, turn up the volume, and let the music make you feel better.

Calm Down One Breath at a Time

Meditation has been used by different cultures around the world for thousands of years and is mostly associated with spiritual development and religious practice. The oldest documented evidence of the practice of meditation is wall art in the Indian subcontinent, which dates from approximately 5,000 to 3,500 BCE. This wall art shows people seated in meditative postures with their eyes half-closed.[38]

While there are many forms of meditation and many ways to arrive at a meditative state, a specific technique called mindfulness has recently become popular and is now widely used across the globe by people of all creeds. Mindfulness generally uses focused breathing to bring the mind's attention to the here and now.

Numerous studies have demonstrated that mindfulness changes the brain in positive ways. In one study, researchers reviewed more than 200 studies of mindfulness and found mindfulness-based therapy was particularly effective for reducing stress, anxiety and depression.[39]

Why not try meditation or mindfulness? Numerous apps and podcasts could help you, so why not do some research until you find one that you like? You could start by trying one of the more popular apps, such as Headspace, Calm, Breathe or Aura.

---

[37] Examined Existence Team. *How Music Changes Your Mood*. Dec 2014. https://examinedexistence.com/how-music-changes-your-mood/

[38] Dienstmann, G. *The History of Meditation*. Blog. https://liveanddare.com/history-of-meditation

[39] Khoury, B., Lecomte, T., Fortin, G., Masse, M., Therien, P., Bouchard, V., Chapleau, M-A, Paquin, K., Hofmann. S. G. (2013) *Mindfulness-based therapy: A comprehensive meta-analysis*, Clinical Psychology Review. Volume 33, Issue 6. Pages 763-771. https://www.sciencedirect.com/science/article/abs/pii/S0272735813000731

So far, we've explored some surface-level strategies for shifting your emotions. Now, it's time to go deeper and discover a more powerful approach—one that leverages System 2 to create lasting emotional change. This technique is called Cognitive Reframing.

8.02 A Technique for Feeling Courageous

Cognitive reframing is a Neuro-Linguistic Programming (NLP) technique that helps you determine the meaning you assign to any situation. By stepping back from events that might otherwise trigger negative emotions, you can prevent them from leading to passive, aggressive, or passive-aggressive behaviour. Instead, cognitive reframing empowers System 2 to take control, allowing you to feel more confident and respond assertively—an approach that increases the likelihood of your Success Cycle flowing in a positive direction and leading to better outcomes.

The meaning you assign to an event is called a frame (think of the phrase *frame of reference*, for example). Reframing provides a new perspective, allowing you to shift how you perceive an event and, in turn, change the meaning you attach to it. If you change the meaning, you change your response.

Remember, meaning isn't inherent—it's something your mind creates, which means it can be changed. But it's up to you to do it! Now, let's explore some real-world examples of reframing.

Artful Politicians: Turning the Tables

Politicians are masters of reframing. No matter what happens, they can spin events in a way that benefits themselves—or discredits their opponents.

> **EXAMPLE: THE PARTYGATE SCANDAL**
>
> In 2022, UK Prime Minister Boris Johnson faced intense scrutiny over a series of social gatherings held at Downing Street during the national lockdowns. The gatherings, held in breach of the very restrictions the government had

imposed on the public, sparked widespread outrage, with many demanding his resignation.

Amid the growing pressure, Johnson appeared before the public and, rather than directly addressing the criticisms, reframed the situation by focusing on the impact of the media coverage. He apologised for the "misjudgement" but immediately shifted attention to the "overblown" nature of the controversy, implying that the media and political opponents were exaggerating the issue. He also highlighted the government's efforts to handle the pandemic, attempting to refocus the narrative on the wider context of national leadership during the crisis.

Through this reframing, Johnson sought to downplay the gravity of his actions and redirect the public's frustration toward the media and political rivals, instead of taking full accountability. The reframing allowed him to maintain some level of political support by shifting the focus away from his personal conduct and onto the media's role in stirring up public anger.

Joking Aside: Reframing Through Humour

Humour is another powerful example of reframing. A well-crafted joke guides your thinking in one direction before unexpectedly shifting the meaning—creating the punchline.

EXAMPLE: A HAIR-RAISING PERSPECTIVE

An elderly woman looked in the mirror one morning and noticed she had just three hairs left on her head. Instead of feeling disheartened, she smiled and said:

"I think I'll braid my hair today."

So, she did—and had a wonderful day.

A few days later, she saw that she had two hairs left. She thought for a moment and said:

"Hmm, two hairs... I fancy a centre parting today."

So, she parted her hair—and had another great day.

A week later, she noticed just one hair remaining. She chuckled and said:

"One hair, huh? I know—a ponytail will be perfect!"

And, once again, she had a fantastic day.

The next morning, she looked in the mirror and saw that she was completely bald. With a big smile, she said:

"Finally bald, huh? How wonderful! I won't have to waste time doing my hair anymore!"

By reframing each stage of hair loss as an opportunity rather than a setback, she maintained a positive outlook—showing how perception shapes experience.

No Ordinary Man: Viktor Frankl's Reframing of Suffering

Few people have faced suffering on the scale that Viktor Frankl did— yet he managed to reframe even the unimaginable horrors he endured.

During World War II, Frankl (1905–1997) spent three years in concentration camps, including Auschwitz and Dachau. He lost his wife, mother, and brother and was subjected to unspeakable suffering. Yet, despite the degradation and misery, Frankl discovered something extraordinary:

"The last of one's freedoms is to choose one's attitude in any given circumstance."

In his book, *Man's Search for Meaning*, Frankl explained how finding meaning in suffering helped some prisoners survive when others did not. He observed that those who accepted their suffering with dignity and found a higher purpose in their pain were more likely to endure.

Frankl later applied this insight to his work as a psychotherapist, teaching people that they alone have the power to define their experiences. His philosophy was simple:

> *"The one thing you can't take away from me is the way I choose to respond to what you do to me."*

Reading about Frankl's experience made me realise that if he could reframe suffering on such a profound level, I could too. What do you think? Could you?

When There's Nothing You Can Do

Reframing is especially powerful when you can't change a situation.

Think back to section 6.02 where we explored assertiveness and considered whether there's anything you can do about a situation. In Step 5, you learned that if the answer is 'no', reframing becomes a valuable tool. When faced with an unchangeable situation you can engage System 2 to consciously shift your perspective, instead of spiralling into frustration and stress, which sends your Success Cycle into a negative direction.

For example, imagine you're stuck on a train due to heavy snow. You could either:

- React negatively: Get frustrated, check the time obsessively, and let stress ruin your mood.

- Reframe the situation: See the delay as extra time to catch up on emails, read a book, or simply relax—so that your evening is free when you get home.

Reframing isn't about blind optimism or ignoring reality. It's about regaining control over your mind—even when circumstances are beyond your control.

How do you apply reframing in your life? Let's explore a simple, step-by-step process.

8.03 A Step-By-Step Process

Step 1: Identify the meaning you're assigning.

Start by noticing the meaning you're attaching to a situation. For example, if you delegate a boring task to a junior colleague, you might think:

"If I delegate this task, it means they'll think I'm being lazy."

Step 2: Generate alternative, positive meanings.

Next, try to come up with as many positive meanings as possible. For instance, delegating a task could also mean:

- I care about their development.
- They're learning something everyone has to do—it's a rite of passage.
- I'm freeing up my time to focus on more important tasks.

Step 3: Choose the meaning that feels most positive to you.

Pick the meaning that empowers you and helps you feel more courageous. The goal is to feel positive so you take action, rather than retreating or self-sabotaging. Reframing should help you develop a more constructive mindset. For example, after hearing a quote from Nelson Mandela, I began to see 'failure' differently. Mandela said, *"I never lose. I either win, or I learn."* Now, I don't beat myself up when things don't work out—I simply learn or win!

Practical Example: How Reframing Works

Let's consider Pierre, who has just found out he's been made redundant. Below are possible ways he could interpret the situation. See if you can think of other meanings, and then choose the one that might help him feel more positive and act in a way that leads to a better outcome in the Success Cycle.

"The fact that I've been made redundant..."

- Means I have a chance to explore new opportunities.
- Could be the push I needed to start my own business.
- Means I can finally focus on something I'm passionate about.
- Is a chance to improve my skills and grow in new ways.

A couple of follow-up questions:

- Did you come up with any other interpretations?
- Which interpretation feels most empowering?

(Spoiler alert: The truth is, all of them could be true—or none of them could be. It's all about the meaning you choose to assign!)

Since none of these interpretations are objectively true, Pierre has the power to choose how to view the situation. If he wants to stay in a positive Success Cycle, he should pick the interpretation that helps him feel positive and motivated.

This approach shows how reframing allows you to shift negative interpretations into something empowering. You can use it for any situation in which you want to change how you feel and behave, ultimately leading to better outcomes.

Don't Deny It

The use of this technique isn't about ignoring your feelings so that you bury them and appear falsely happy. It's about harnessing System 2 to consciously change your feelings in the moment so that you are in control of them rather than *them* being in control of *you*. If you can change how you're feeling at any moment, you'll have more chance to choose your *response* rather than *reacting* with a knee-jerk action: you can change your behaviour to achieve more positive outcomes in your life.

For any chronic event that trigger powerful emotions, it's important to acknowledge and deal with your emotions, especially those stemming from loss, grief, or bereavement. A sad fact is that many people will face distressing events at some point in their life, from death and illness to redundancy and divorce. No matter how hard you might wish, there is often nothing you can do to avoid or change them: a change in your behaviour, feelings or thoughts can't alter the outcome. A loved one may still be dead, or gravely ill; you may still have been made redundant; your partner still wants a divorce.

Needless to say, this book is not intended to replace professional counselling. However, you may well find that some of the ideas set out here are still relevant when it comes to living through emotionally challenging times.

If you realise that you, or a loved one, is struggling to let go of a strong emotion, and upon reading Elisabeth Kübler-Ross's book, *On Death and Dying*, you appreciate that you need further help, you could talk about your feelings to a friend, family member, health professional or counsellor. If you live in the UK, the NHS website provides details on seeking further help: www.nhs.uk/conditions/stress-anxiety-depression/coping-with-bereavement. In the UK, Samaritans (https://www.samaritans.org/) provides free, confidential listening support via phone or email; their phone lines are open all day, every day. Outside of the UK, support similar to Samaritans is offered in many countries; you can find out more via the Befrienders International network,

www.befrienders.org.

Although you can use reframing to change any feeling, this chapter promised to help you feel more courageous. So, let's look at how you can use reframing to be bolder at work.

8.04 Reframing: Practice with General Examples

To be more courageous, you might have realised that there were already some useful reframes in Chapter 7. To save you looking back, below are the 'no' answers to the questions in Activity 1c. Notice how they are all reframes! Why not borrow these reframes to help make yourself feel more courageous?

1. **Do you fear public speaking?**

   No. You might get nervous for the first few minutes but then you feel alive. Presentations are an opportunity to share your thoughts and ideas with a captive audience!

2. **Do you fear failure?**

   No. You don't believe in failure. You never want to regret not trying something; you would rather regret having tried it. In the words of Susan Jeffers: 'Feel the fear and do it anyway'. (And, of course, there's the one I 'borrowed' from Nelson Mandela: 'There is no such thing as failure: I either win or learn.')

3. **Do you fear change?**

   No. You think life is boring without change so you embrace it. After all: 'change is the only constant'!

4. **Do you fear not being good enough?**

   No. You know it's impossible to be good at everything so you accept what you are good at, and work on what you would like to be better at.

5. **Do you fear not being liked?**

   No. You know it's impossible to be liked by everyone. As long as you treat others the way you would like to be treated, it's up to them to choose if they like you or not.

6. **Do you fear losing control?**

   No. You know control is but an illusion, so you have no problem letting go.

If none of these reframes resonate with you, try looking at how others reframe the specific fear you'd like to overcome. One of their perspectives might work better for you. The key is to engage System 2 and find a reframe that instantly changes how you feel, enabling you to be courageous and no longer allow fear to hold you back from success.

Now that you're familiar with reframing, it's time to put it into practice with your own work scenarios.

8.05 Reframing: Practice with Your Own Objectives

In Activity 14 (Chapter 7), you reflected on the meanings you assign to each of your objectives. You've already completed Steps 1–3. Now it's time to move on to Step 4, where you'll brainstorm reframes for each of your objectives.

Activity 15: Reframing Your Objectives

Step 1: Revisit Your Objectives

- *Example*: I want to be able to give feedback, but I tend to keep quiet.

Step 2: Identify the Emotional Impact

- *Example*: When I don't give feedback, I feel frustrated.

Step 3: Understand the Meaning You Assign

- *Example*: If I were to give feedback, I might upset the other person.

Step 4: Reframe the Meaning

- *Example*: If I were to give feedback, I'd be offering that person an opportunity to grow.

Activity 15 - Sam's Reflections & Reframes:

1. Getting Muhammed to do what I ask

- **Self-Sabotaging Behaviour:** Avoid speaking to him about his behaviour.

- **How I Feel:** Fine, because I've already had an assertive conversation with him.
- **What It Means to Me:** The issue has been addressed, so I don't need to discover the meaning or reframe it.

2. **Speaking up and sharing my ideas in meetings**
- **Self-Sabotaging Behaviour:** I keep quiet.
- **How I Feel:** Angry and frustrated.
- **What It Means to Me:** I worry that I might say something silly.
- **Reframe:** Just as I could say something silly, I could also say something valuable that helps the team.

3. **Shouting about my strengths**
- **Self-Sabotaging Behaviour:** I downplay my abilities.
- **How I Feel:** Uncomfortable.
- **What It Means to Me:** If people expect too much from me, I might disappoint them.
- **Reframe:** Stating the facts about my strengths is not about setting high expectations—it's about being honest about what I'm capable of.

4. **Speaking to Belle about my colleagues not doing their fair share**
- **Self-Sabotaging Behaviour:** I avoid speaking to Belle and do the extra work myself.
- **How I Feel:** Fine, because I've had an assertive conversation with her.
- **What It Means to Me:** I've already taken action, so I don't need to dwell on it.
- **Reframe:** I've done the right thing. It's now up to others to step up.

5. **Doing new tasks outside my comfort zone**
- **Self-Sabotaging Behaviour:** I avoid new tasks.
- **How I Feel:** Stressed.
- **What It Means to Me:** If I fail, people will think I'm an imposter.
- **Reframe:** I have successfully faced new challenges my entire life. This is no different.

6. **Delivering last-minute presentations**
- **Self-Sabotaging Behaviour:** I make excuses to avoid them.
- **How I Feel:** Terrified.
- **What It Means to Me:** If I don't prepare enough, I might say something wrong, and people will think I'm not capable.
- **Reframe:** I might also say something insightful that impresses people.

7. **Switching off from work**
- **Self-Sabotaging Behaviour:** I work in the middle of the night.
- **How I Feel:** Exhausted.
- **What It Means to Me:** If I don't stay on top of everything, people will think I'm not capable.
- **Reframe:** Working at night makes me less productive the next day. By resting properly, I'll actually be more efficient.

8. **Letting go and moving on when things don't go well**
- **Self-Sabotaging Behaviour:** I focus on what I did wrong.
- **How I Feel:** Stressed.
- **What It Means to Me:** If I made a mistake, it means I'm not good enough.

- **Reframe:** One mistake does not define me. I can learn from it and do better next time.

Chapter Summary

Every day, as events unfold around you, you respond to your internal 'map' of reality, rather than to objective reality. Since this happens outside of your conscious awareness, it follows that System 1 is responsible for assigning meaning. When System 1 assigns an empowering meaning, it drives the Success Cycle in a positive direction, making you feel courageous, behave assertively, and achieve positive outcomes. However, when it assigns a limiting meaning, it drives the Success Cycle in a negative direction, making you feel fearful, behave non-assertively, and achieve negative outcomes.

While there are various techniques you can use to change how you feel in an instant—such as adjusting your language, laughing, or listening to music—there's also a more complex approach: Cognitive Reframing. Since there's no inherent meaning in any situation, and you are responding to your map of reality rather than to objective reality, it's possible to engage System 2 to assign empowered, conscious meanings to events in your life. This gives you the freedom to choose how you respond.

It's not about ignoring problems but rather having the flexibility to make your mind work *for* you, rather than *against* you. The key takeaway is that, whichever technique you choose, you have the power to change how you feel and become more courageous.

What's Next?

Now that you have a better understanding of the feeling part of the cycle, let's dive deeper into the source of those feelings: the thinking part of the Success Cycle. Understanding this will show you how to build greater resilience. This section will be divided into two parts: the first focuses on the science behind your thoughts, while the second equips you with the skills to think more positively and bounce back from challenges with greater strength.

9

THE SCIENCE OF RESILIENCE: BOUNCING BACK STRONGER

"Our greatest glory is not in never falling, but in rising every time we fall."
Confucius[40]

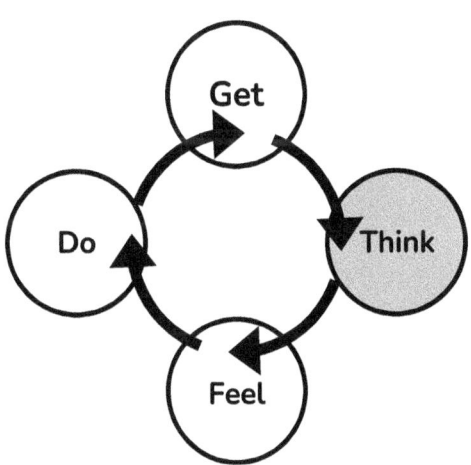

Sam has new-found admiration for her manager, Belle, and appreciates Belle's efforts in helping her to gain more experience, knowledge and skills so she can progress to the

---

[40] *Confucius was a renowned philosopher, politician, and educator who lived in ancient China. His teachings today are known as Confucianism.*

role of Project Manager. Sam knows she has to do the last-minute presentation—not because Belle wants her to, but because it will help to achieve her goal of a promotion.

Even though she knows it's for her own benefit, and even after she's reminded herself that she might say some good stuff too (reframing from the last chapter), when Sam tries to practice the presentation, she can't because a little voice in her head—her 'self-talk'—keeps interrupting her, saying that she won't be as good as Belle, she'll make a fool of herself, or that everyone will judge her if she can't answer questions from the team.

These thoughts spark images in her mind's eye of looking stupid and saying something silly in front of everyone, while being convinced that they judge her performance to be pathetic because they're used to Belle's flawless presentations. These thoughts make Sam feel so uncomfortable that she decides it's better not to do the presentation: she would rather not have a go than risk the embarrassment.

Resilience is the result of thinking about challenges (and set-backs) in a specific way. You can clearly see a *lack* of resilience in the above example: it's not Sam's ability that stops her from doing the last-minute presentation, but rather her thoughts, and the corresponding voice in her head. In other words, Sam's thoughts about a specific challenge overwhelm her to the point of making her give up.

So, what would resilience have looked like? Sam would have demonstrated resilience by giving it a go, despite her thoughts. It would have demonstrated resolve and determination—trying something she found find difficult despite the potential professional risks. (Of course, that's not to say you would do absolutely *anything* in pursuit of demonstrating resilience: you would need to do a cost-benefit analysis first! In this scenario, if Sam did the presentation and her worst fears came true, so what? Her team is more likely to be proud of her for giving it a go and making a few mistakes than ridicule her for the mistakes she might have made.)

Notice that Sam's lack of resilience ensures she doesn't gain any experience of delivering presentations when she doesn't have time to prepare. Without this experience, she will not get better at them, and will not be promoted. In short, it's Sam's lack of resilience that causes the Success Cycle to flow in a negative direction, and prevents her from getting what she wants.

What This Chapter Covers:

- 9.01 Assessing Your Resilience
- 9.02 Everyday Signs of Struggling with Resilience
- 9.03 Common Self-Talk Themes
- 9.04 Why Does Negative Thinking Dominate?
- 9.05 How Your Thoughts Are Generalised
- 9.06 How Your Thoughts Are Deleted
- 9.07 How Your Thoughts Are Distorted

9.01 Assessing Your Resilience

Take this short assessment to reflect on your current level of resilience. Read each pair of statements and choose the one that best describes how you typically think and react. Be honest: this is about where you are now, not where you wish to be.

1. **When faced with problems, I:**
    - **A:** see obstacles everywhere.
    - **B:** see opportunities to learn and grow.
2. **When I experience failure, I:**
    - **A:** feel stuck and discouraged.
    - **B:** view it as a learning experience.
3. **In difficult situations, I:**
    - **A:** struggle to think clearly.

- B: stay calm and look for solutions.

4. **When things change unexpectedly, I:**
    - A: find it difficult to adapt.
    - B: embrace flexibility and adjust.

5. **When I encounter a problem, I:**
    - A: feel like giving up.
    - B: take proactive steps to solve it.

6. **My approach to taking action is:**
    - A: to procrastinate unless I'm forced to act.
    - B: to show initiative and move towards my goals.

7. **When something negative happens, I:**
    - A: dwell on it and struggle to move past it.
    - B: focus on what I can control and take action.

8. **When I think about the future, I:**
    - A: worry about what could go wrong.
    - B: look forward with optimism.

9. **When faced with uncertainty, I:**
    - A: doubt my ability to cope.
    - B: trust that I can handle whatever comes my way.

10. **When approaching challenges, I:**
    - A: prefer sticking to the familiar way of doing things.
    - B: am open to trying new approaches.

11. **When major change happens, I:**

    ○ A: struggle to think clearly.

    ○ B: use it as an opportunity to re-evaluate what's important.

12. **When reflecting on my past, I:**

    ○ A: remember failures more than successes.

    ○ B: celebrate successes and learn from setbacks.

Your Resilience Score

Count how many times you chose A versus B.

- **Mostly Bs?** You already have a resilient mindset and demonstrate behaviours that help you adapt and thrive in times of change.

- **Mostly As?** This may indicate that resilience is an area for growth—but don't be discouraged! Resilience is a skill that can be developed at any stage of life.

As you move through this chapter, you'll discover practical strategies to shift your thinking, build resilience, and become more adaptable in any situation.

9.02 Everyday Signs of Struggling with Resilience

Resilience is the ability to bounce back from setbacks, adapt to change, and keep moving forward despite challenges. Your mindset plays a crucial role in how well you handle adversity. When resilience is lacking, the key to developing it lies in recognising that how you think about challenges is central. The way you think determines how you interpret a problem, which then influences whether you feel courageous or fearful.

As you discovered in the last chapter, when you feel courageous, you're more likely to take positive, adaptive action. But if you feel fearful, it triggers reactive behaviours, leaving you less equipped to address the issue constructively. So how can you uncover what you're really thinking?

One effective approach is to become aware of the internal 'chatter' in your head—the ongoing conversations you have with yourself. This is often known as self-talk, your internal dialogue, or your inner voice. Common sense would suggest that self-talk is an expression of your thoughts, so a logical conclusion is that we can examine our thoughts by paying attention to what we're saying to ourselves inside our mind.

The problem is that there is a *lot* of chatter going on inside your mind.[41] So, how do you know what to pay attention to and what to ignore in order to become more resilient? To find out, let's look at the most common types of self-talk:

- *Instructional*: your self-talk reminds you to do something: 'Remember to withdraw £20 to pay back Eliza'. Or it gives you step-by-step breakdown of how to do something: 'First I must read the instructions, then lay out each component, and check all the pieces are there...'

- *Conversational*: your self-talk is basically having a chat with itself: 'What do you think? I think it's a really good idea. How about you? I'm not so sure. Why?'

- *Motivational*: your self-talk gives you a pep talk to psych you up before an important event: 'Come on, you can do this.' Or it congratulates you afterwards for giving something your best shot: 'Brilliant! Well done for trying!'

- *Demotivational*: your self-talk chastises you for doing something wrong, or berates and criticises you: 'You idiot! What did you do that for?'

We're most interested in identifying motivational and demotivational self-talk because these thoughts directly influence your feelings. Motivational self-talk acts like an internal cheerleader,

---

[41] *Estimates vary from twenty thousand to eighty thousand thoughts per day. So, even if we take a more conservative view and opt for the lower end of this range, we still have a lot of thoughts whirring around our heads: twenty-thousand thoughts per twelve hour period equates to roughly 28 thoughts per minute.*

boosting your courage and helping you tackle challenges head-on. In contrast, demotivational self-talk acts as an internal critic, feeding fear and self-doubt.

The voice that dominates your thoughts in a given situation can make all the difference between success and failure. This is because your thoughts influence your feelings, which then shape the flow of the Success Cycle. In turn, this affects your behaviour (what you do) and the outcomes you achieve.

You can better understand and manage your thoughts if you categorise your self-talk as motivational if it makes you feel positive, or demotivational if it makes you feel negative.

We could label the self-talk that gives you a running commentary on your day, or reminds you to do things, or plans and organises what you're going to do, as neutral because it is unlikely to impact your feelings positively or negatively. The only time it might be negative is if it becomes so obsessive that it causes stress and blocks out room for any other type of thinking. Most of the time, though, this type of self-talk simply helps you think about and understand the events in your life.

It is important to classify your self-talk according to the feelings it elicits (positive, neutral, or negative) because self-talk is not black and white: it's all down to what the self-talk means to you as an individual, and how it impacts you.

For example, suppose Belle gives Sam a presentation to do in three weeks' time. The same self-talk is there ('You'll make a fool of yourself'), but this time it's motivational because it will make her prepare and practice until she feels super-confident to do the presentation. (This is what happened when Sam had a positive experience of presenting to important stakeholders in Chapter 2.)

The important thing to remember is that, despite Sam's self-talk *appearing* negative, it is positive in the context of having enough time to prepare. The key is to understand how it makes you feel and what behaviour it creates.

Of course, you could *reframe* a thought that's made you feel negative, but this chapter offers another method for interrupting System 1's default mode by consciously changing your thoughts—the chat inside your head—before the feelings have even formed. By doing so, you can boost your resilience.

9.03 Common Self-Talk Themes

Do you ever find yourself engaged in internal dialogues that sap your motivation instead of boosting it? Take a moment to reflect on how these thoughts might be shaping your mindset and driving the Success Cycle in a negative direction. To help you identify these patterns, consider whether you answer 'yes' to any of the following questions about common types of self-talk:

- Do you often criticise yourself excessively when things don't go as planned? For instance, if you forget an important meeting, do you immediately think, "I'm such an idiot"?
- Do you frequently compare yourself to others, thinking, "He's so much more talented than I am"?
- Do you set unrealistically high expectations for yourself and feel disheartened when you don't meet them?
- Do you assume others are judging you, telling yourself things like "They probably think I'm lazy"?
- Do you tend to magnify your perceived shortcomings, thinking, "I always stumble over my words in presentations"?
- Do you blow minor setbacks out of proportion, telling yourself, "This mistake could cost me my job"?

> **Sam's Response:** *"Most of these common types of self-talk sound familiar to me! It's no wonder I give up so easily when I'm constantly pressuring myself to be 'perfect' while comparing myself to others and magnifying my flaws. I often think, 'I'll probably embarrass myself!' Now I realise why I*

struggle with resilience: my negative thoughts lead me to give up too easily."

Like Sam, did you recognise that some of your self-talk discourages you from taking action? If so, it might make you more likely to quit or exert minimal effort. The result is that you reinforce the thought that 'I can't do it', which ultimately undermines your resilience. (Of course, some people may find motivation in being told they can't do something. Personally, I thrive on challenges: when someone says I can't achieve something, it fuels my determination to prove them wrong!)

Conversely, if you've discovered that your self-talk encourages you to believe in your abilities, you may be more inclined to try new things. When your self-talk reinforces the notion that you can succeed, you'll find yourself proving that belief true and, in turn, becoming more resilient. (It's also possible to tell yourself you can succeed, only to face setbacks. While you may not achieve your desired outcome, these experiences can still strengthen your resilience.)

If many of these self-talk patterns resonated with you, there's no need to feel discouraged—you're not alone. Many people grapple with negative self-talk. Let's explore why this might be the case.

9.04 Why Does Negative Thinking Dominate?

Thinking more negatively than positively simply means you're human! You are programmed to think negatively due to what psychologists call *negativity bias*, which describes the way we tend to be more heavily influenced by negative experiences than positive ones. It is thought that this trait evolved as a survival instinct millions of years ago, when humans focused more on avoiding potential threats than on rewards. In keeping with Charles Darwin's notion of the survival of the fittest, it was the people who paid a lot of attention to danger who survived long enough to reproduce, thereby passing this 'survival instinct' trait to the next generation. As such, our ancestors left us with a brain that is primed to focus on negative experiences rather than positive ones.

Nobel Prize winner Daniel Kahneman said: "This asymmetry between the power of positive and negative expectations or experiences has an evolutionary history. Organisms that treat threats as more urgent than opportunities have a better chance to survive and reproduce." [42]

The relative power of positive versus negative experience has been studied by the psychologist John Cacioppo, Ph.D. Cacioppo showed people pictures that would invoke either positive, negative, or neutral feelings while simultaneously recording the electrical activity in the brain's cerebral cortex to give a measure of the magnitude of information processing taking place. He found that the brain reacts more strongly—he measured a greater surge in electrical activity—in response to stimuli it deems negative than those it deems positive. According to an article in *Psychology Today*, then, "Our attitudes are more heavily influenced by downbeat news than good news." [43]

To make matters worse, there is another reason why you are likely to feel loss more acutely than gain. It's due to something called *loss aversion*. Imagine I offered you a bet: I am going to toss a coin, and if it lands on heads, I will give you £150. But if it lands on tails, *you* will have to give *me* £100. Would you take the bet? Chances are, you wouldn't—according, at least, to Daniel Kahneman. Kahneman demonstrated that the human mind is naturally attuned to feeling loss more acutely than gain, and to agonise over risk rather than relish opportunity.

Kahneman explained "The rejection of this gamble is an act of System 2 but the critical inputs are emotional responses that are generated by System 1 . For most people, the fear of losing £100 is more intense than the hope of gaining £150. We concluded from many such observations that 'losses loom larger than gain' and that people are *loss averse*." [44]

---

[42] Kahneman, D. (2012) *Thinking Fast & Slow*. Penguin.

[43] Estroff Marano, H. (2003). Our Brain's Negative Bias. Psychology Today. https://www.psychologytoday.com/us/articles/200306/our-brains-negative-bias

[44] Kahneman, D. (2012) *Thinking, Fast & Slow*. Penguin

Given that System 1's default mode is to focus more on negative experiences and perceive loss more intensely, it is no wonder so many people struggle with resilience! But that doesn't mean you're powerless—far from it. Before we explore how to change your self-talk, we first need to understand how your thoughts are filtered and how this process influences you.

Thoughts Shape Reality

I explained in Chapter 3 how your brain filters the vast amount of information it receives from the external world by deleting, distorting, and generalising it—much like an internet search engine, showing only what it thinks is relevant. The same process applies to your thoughts: by the time they reach your conscious awareness as self-talk, they have already been filtered, altered, and shaped without you even realising it. This means your thoughts aren't absolute truths—they are interpretations based on the way your mind has processed information. These interpretations then lead to assumptions, which can either help or hinder you.

Now, consider what you learned in Chapter 7: people respond to their map of reality, not to reality. Your brain interprets self-talk in a way that reinforces what you already think—yet this self-talk, and the negative emotions it triggers, rarely reflects reality. (It's worth noting that even self-talk that creates positive emotions isn't necessarily grounded in reality—but since this benefits you and supports the Success Cycle, it's not something we want to change!)

So how can you recognise when your self-talk has been deleted, distorted, or generalised? One powerful tool is the Meta Model[45], a set of questions designed to challenge and clarify the meaning of your thoughts. The Meta Model helps reconnect missing details, uncover

---

[45] *The Meta Model was the first NLP model to be developed by John Grinder and Richard Bandler (adapted from ideas originated by linguist Noam Chomsky) after they modelled the therapists Virginia Satir and Fritz Perls. Combined with John Grinder's transformational grammar research, they published their results 'The Structure of Magic Volume 1' (Science and Behaviour Books, 1975). The name Meta Model came about because 'meta' means 'above' or 'beyond' so the Meta Model is a model of language on language, clarifying language by using language itself. The Meta Model consists of 13 patterns divided into three categories: Deletions, Distortions and Generalisations.*

distortions, and break unhelpful generalisations, allowing you to see your thoughts more rationally and objectively.

Let's start with generalisation.

9.05 How Your Thoughts Are Generalised

For this, we'll focus on three key ways in which your mind generalises the information around you:

- Modal Operator of Necessity: rigid rules and expectations that create a sense of pressure.
- Modal Operator of Possibility: assumptions about what is or isn't possible.
- Universal Quantifiers: sweeping simplifications that exaggerate situations, making them seem bigger than they are.

Modal Operator of Necessity

Modal Operator of Necessity are the self-imposed rules that dictate what you believe is required or appropriate. They often appear in self-talk as words like 'should', 'must', or 'have to'.

For example:

- "I should always be productive."
- "I must never make mistakes."
- "I have to be perfect at this."

The issue with Modal Operator of Necessity is that they create a sense of rigid obligation, increasing stress and pressure. When your inner dialogue insists, "I must finish this project perfectly," it leaves no room for flexibility, learning, or adapting to challenges. This kind of thinking can make tasks feel overwhelming and can lead to unnecessary anxiety, procrastination, or burnout.

Modal Operator of Possibility

Modal Operator of Possibility shape what you believe is possible or impossible, often appearing as words like 'can', 'can't', 'possible', and 'impossible'. These phrases influence whether you take action or give up before even trying.

For example:

- "I can't learn new skills at my age."
- "It's impossible to find a job I enjoy."
- "I'll never be able to run a marathon."

The danger of Modal Operator of Possibility is that they set self-imposed limitations. When you tell yourself, "I can't do this," you reinforce the idea that success is out of reach, making you less likely to put in effort. Over time, these thoughts become self-fulfilling prophecies.

Universal Quantifiers

Universal Quantifiers are generalisations that exaggerate experiences, making isolated events seem like unchangeable patterns. They typically include words like 'always', 'never', 'everyone', and 'everything'.

- For example:
- "I always get overlooked."
- "Everything I do goes wrong."
- "Nobody ever listens to me."

The problem with Universal Quantifiers is that they distort reality by turning a single event into an unbreakable rule. If you say, "I always fail," your mind filters out evidence of past successes, reinforcing a belief that may not be true.

Now that we've explored how your mind generalises information, we'll turn to another cognitive filter: deletions—the details your mind leaves out—and how they influence your thinking and decision-making.

9.06 How Your Thoughts Are Deleted

The process of deletion occurs when essential details are omitted from thoughts or statements, leaving them vague and open to interpretation. This can lead to confusion and misjudgement. By identifying and challenging these deletions, you can gain greater clarity, improve resilience, and make more informed decisions.

There are three main types of deletion in self-talk:

- Simple Deletion: when key details are missing, making a statement ambiguous.
- Unspecified Verbs: when the action being described is unclear.
- Comparative Deletion: when an incomplete comparison leads to distorted thinking.

Simple Deletion

A Simple Deletion occurs when part of a thought is left out, making it unclear or incomplete. The missing details can lead to confusion or unnecessary stress, as the mind fills in the gaps—often in a negative way.

Examples:

- "It's important." (What is important? Why is it important?)
- "I feel uncomfortable." (Uncomfortable about what? How?)
- "I need to do this." (What exactly do you need to do? By when? Why?)

The problem with Simple Deletion is that it creates vague self-talk. If you tell yourself, "I need to fix this," but don't define what needs fixing or how you plan to do it, the lack of detail can make the task seem overwhelming. This ambiguity can cause procrastination or unnecessary anxiety.

Unspecified Verbs

Unspecified Verbs occur when an action is described vaguely, making it unclear what actually happened or how it affected you. This can make it difficult to address problems, communicate effectively, or take meaningful action.

Examples:

- "He hurt me." (How? Physically? Emotionally? Through words or actions?)
- "I handled that badly." (What exactly did you do? What part was handled badly?)
- "I created a bad impression on them." (In what way? Did they say something, or are you assuming?)

The issue with Unspecified Verbs is that they can make events seem worse than they actually are. If you tell yourself, "I handled that badly," without specifying what went wrong, you risk reinforcing self-doubt instead of learning from the experience.

Comparative Deletion

Comparative Deletions happen when a comparison is made, but the standard of comparison is left out. This leads to incomplete or distorted thinking, often fuelling feelings of inadequacy.

Examples:

- "She's better than me." (Better at what? In what context? According to whom?)
- "That is easier." (Easier than what? For whom?)
- "I did that badly." (Compared to what standard? Your past performance? Someone else's?)

Comparative Deletion reinforces negative self-perceptions by making generalised judgements without clear reference points. If you think, "She's better than me," but don't specify what you're comparing, you might end up feeling inferior for no valid reason.

Now that we've explored how deletion affects self-talk, we'll move on to the final cognitive filter, distortion—through which thoughts become twisted versions of reality. By recognising these patterns, you'll be able to challenge unhelpful thinking and build a more accurate and resilient mindset.

9.07 How Your Thoughts Are Distorted

The Reticular Activating System (RAS) also filters information through distortion, a process through which thoughts are twisted or assumptions are made without evidence. We'll explore four key types of distortion:

- Mind-Reading
- Nominalisation
- Cause-Effect
- Complex Equivalence.

Mind Reading

This distortion occurs when someone assumes they know what others are thinking or feeling without concrete evidence. In self-talk, this pattern often leads to unnecessary worry, anxiety, or self-doubt because the assumptions are usually negative and unfounded. Mind Reading distorts reality by creating conclusions based on speculation rather than facts.

Common examples include:

- "They don't like me."
- "He thinks I'm an idiot."
- "She wishes I wasn't working on this project."

The issue with Mind Reading is that it leads you to act in ways that unintentionally confirm your assumption, even if it was completely incorrect. For example, if you assume a colleague is upset with you because they didn't greet you warmly in the morning, you might avoid them for the rest of the day. This could make them feel distant or even annoyed, reinforcing your thoughts that they're upset—even though their behaviour may have had nothing to do with you in the first place.

Nominalisation

This occurs when verbs, which are dynamic processes, are turned into nouns, which are static concepts. They create a sense of rigidity because they present fluid processes as if they were fixed entities.

Examples include:

- "The stress" (notice this is presented as a noun but it's from the verb to be stressed).
- "The communication" (notice this is presented as a noun but it's from the verb to communicate).
- "The fear" (notice this is presented as a noun but it's from the verb to fear).

The problem with Nominalisation is that it can make an issue feel permanent and unchangeable, leading you to believe there's no point in taking action to address that issue. If you say, "The stress is making me ill," the word 'stress' is abstract and feels like an uncontrollable force, making it difficult to do anything about it.

Cause-Effect

This refers to statements in which one thing is said to automatically cause another, often without clear evidence or acknowledgment of other factors. This pattern is common in self-talk and can lead to disempowering thoughts, such as feeling controlled by external circumstances or internal emotions.

For example:

- "They make me feel unimportant."
- "I can't succeed because of my past."
- "If I fail, everyone will think I'm useless."

The problem with Cause-Effect is that it can lead you to oversimplify complex situations, attributing a single cause to an outcome when multiple factors may be involved. If you say, "The meeting went poorly because I didn't speak up," you might overlook other factors, like poor planning, unclear objectives, or other team members not speaking up, which also contributed to the outcome. This narrow Cause-Effect thinking can prevent you from addressing *all* the underlying issues.

Complex Equivalence

Complex Equivalence happens when two unrelated things are treated as if they automatically mean the same thing. This distortion can lead to limiting ideas, where a single event is wrongly interpreted as evidence of something much bigger or more negative.

Examples:

- "He didn't say thank you, so he must not appreciate me."
- "I stumbled over my words, which means I'm terrible at public speaking."
- "She disagreed with me, so she must not respect my opinion."

The problem with Complex Equivalence is that it locks you into fixed interpretations that may not be accurate. For example, believing "If I make a mistake, it means I'm a failure" equates imperfection with incompetence, even though mistakes are an essential part of learning and growth. This type of distortion can make setbacks feel overwhelming rather than manageable.

Knowing that your thoughts and self-talk have been severely deleted, distorted and generalised without your conscious awareness is hugely empowering because once you recognise these patterns, you can challenge them by engaging System 2. In this way, you can develop more accurate, balanced and resilient thoughts, which will help to ensure your Success Cycle flows in a positive direction.

Now that you know how thoughts are filtered through deletion, distortion, and generalisation, it's time to put your knowledge into practice. Below is an activity to help you deepen your understanding of the Meta Model.

Activity 16: Spot the Thinking Trap

Below are the six common examples of self-talk you encountered earlier. Your task is to identify which Meta Model pattern each one belongs to.

Read each statement carefully and decide whether it represents:

- Mind Reading (assuming you know what others think or feel)
- Complex Equivalence (equating two unrelated things as if they mean the same)
- Cause-Effect (believing one event automatically causes another)
- Modal Operator of Necessity (self-imposed rules about what must or should happen)
- Universal Quantifiers (broad, exaggerated statements)
- Comparative Deletion (making comparisons without specifying what is being compared)

Try it now! Match each statement to the correct Meta Model pattern:

1. "I'm such an idiot."
2. "He's so much more talented than I am."
3. "I must always meet my own high standards."
4. "They probably think I'm lazy."
5. "I always stumble over my words in presentations."
6. "This mistake could cost me my job."

Once you've completed the activity, you'll find the correct answers and explanations below.

Spoiler Alert: Here are the answers

1. **"I'm such an idiot."** → Complex Equivalence

- This statement assumes that making a mistake (one event) means you are fundamentally an idiot (a broader conclusion). However, forgetting a meeting or making an error does not define who you are, your level of intelligence, or self-worth.

2. **"He's so much more talented than I am."** → Comparative Deletion

- This is a comparison, but what specific qualities or skills are being compared? In what way is the other person more talented? Without details, this vague statement can reinforce feelings of inadequacy.

3. **"I must always meet my own high standards."** → Modal Operator of Necessity

- The use of 'must' creates a rigid rule, implying that failing to meet high standards is unacceptable. This kind of thinking can cause unnecessary pressure and stress.

4. **"They probably think I'm lazy."** → Mind Reading

- This assumes you know what others think without any real evidence. It fuels anxiety and self-doubt, leading you to act on imagined judgements instead of reality.

5. **"I always stumble over my words in presentations."** → Universal Quantifier

- The word 'always' suggests that this is a constant, unchanging truth. In reality, you may not stumble every time, but this exaggeration can make the problem feel permanent.

6. "This mistake could cost me my job." → Cause-Effect

- This statement assumes that one mistake directly leads to job loss, without considering other factors such as overall job performance, workplace policies, or past successes.

Now you have a little practice under your belt, see if you can identify which Meta Model patterns you use.

Activity 17: Your Mental Shortcuts: Recognising the Impact of Mental Shortcuts on Your Objectives

1. **Refer to Your Objectives:** Reflect on areas where mental shortcuts may be affecting your resilience.

2. **Analyse Your Self-Talk:** Consider thoughts such as, *"I want to [objective], but I can't because I think [self-talk]…"*

3. **Label the Shortcut:** Identify whether the thought involves a deletion, distortion, or generalisation. You might notice more than one pattern at play.

<u>Activity 17– Sam's Answer:</u>

- **Objective:** I want to be able to switch off from work.
- **Self-Talk:** *"I must keep on top of my workload."*
- **Shortcut Identified:**
  - *Modal Operator of Necessity:* The idea that something *must* be done creates unnecessary pressure.

—

- **Objective:** I want to let go and move on when things don't go well.
- **Self-Talk:** *"How have I messed up?"*
- **Shortcut Identified:**
  - *Complex Equivalence:* Assuming that if something goes wrong, it automatically *means I* have messed up.

—

- **Objective:** I want to feel comfortable delivering last-minute presentations.
- **Self-Talk:** *"I'm scared of everyone judging me."*
- **Shortcut Identified:**
  - *Universal Quantifier:* Assuming that *everyone* will judge me.
  - *Unspecified Verb:* Failing to specify *what* aspects everyone might be evaluating, leading to a vague and exaggerated fear.
  - *Complex Equivalence:* Thinking that delivering last-minute presentations *means* that I'll be judged.

Chapter Summary

Your thoughts shape your reality by influencing whether the Success Cycle flows in a positive or negative direction. However, your thoughts are filtered before you even become consciously aware of them—they have been deleted, distorted, and generalised, meaning your perception of reality may not be as accurate as you assume.

By examining the Meta Model, a set of language patterns from Neuro-Linguistic Programming (NLP), you can begin to recognise how your mind has twisted information, leading to self-imposed barriers. By understanding these patterns you can see how much of your thinking is based on assumptions rather than facts.

What's Next?

Being aware of, and being able to identify, the deletions, distortions, and generalisations in your thinking is incredibly powerful. Until now, these mental filters have been shaping assumptions outside of your conscious awareness, leading you to experience a reality that doesn't align with what you truly want. In the next chapter, you'll learn how to challenge and shift these filters by consciously engaging System 2 thinking to ensure you can face any difficulty with resilience.

BUILDING RESILIENCE:
KEY SKILLS FOR ENDURANCE AND GROWTH

"A few people are born resilient. The rest of us need to work consciously at developing our abilities."[46]
Dr. Al Siebert

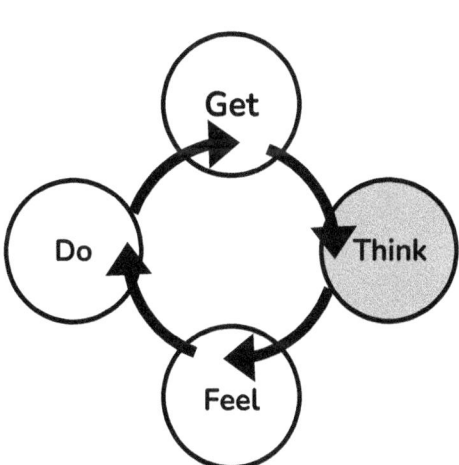

Upon realising that her self-talk is the key barrier to delivering last-minute presentations, Sam feels a surge of excitement. She's eager to learn how to challenge the

---

[46] Dr. Al Siebert was founder and director of The Resiliency Centre. His best-selling book, The Resiliency Advantage, won the Independent Publisher's 2006 Best Self Help Book Award.

deletions, distortions, and generalisations contained in her thoughts. By engaging System 2 and questioning her thoughts, she won't just step up for Belle—she'll also harness the Success Cycle to her advantage, increasing her chances of securing the Project Manager promotion she's been striving for. This newfound awareness marks a pivotal turning point in her professional growth.

In this chapter, you'll learn how to consciously engage System 2 to challenge the mental shortcuts that are holding you back from being your most resilient self. As you discover the techniques, you'll find that the more you challenge your mental filters in your self-talk, the more control you have over your responses. Instead of feeling overwhelmed by challenges or stuck in negative patterns, you'll be able to be more resilient, see opportunities, make better decisions, and take purposeful action, ensuring your Success Cycle flows in a positive direction.

What This Chapter Covers:

- 10.01 Silencing Your Inner Critic
- 10.02 Challenging Generalisations
- 10.03 Challenging Deletions
- 10.04 Challenging Distortions

10.01 Silencing Your Inner Critic

In section 9.03, you explored common examples of self-talk. Recognising your internal dialogue is a powerful first step, as it can either propel you forward or hold you back. When your self-talk acts as your harshest critic, it can drive the Success Cycle in a negative direction, leaving you perplexed as to why you keep self-sabotaging and achieving the opposite of what you want.

Before diving into the specific technique of how to challenge Meta Model patterns, let's explore some simple yet effective ways to be more objective when facing your inner critic.

Do you often criticise yourself excessively when things don't go as planned? For instance, if you forget an important meeting, do you immediately think, "I'm such an idiot"?

Instead of internalising negative messages, be curious about the positive intention behind your negative self-talk. For example, if it's telling you that you're an idiot, consider what it's really trying to achieve—perhaps it's trying to toughen you up or protect your ego. Look at the evidence: Was it really your fault? Are you truly incompetent, or did you simply make a mistake that you can learn from? Stubbing your toe doesn't make you an idiot; it may just mean you need to be more aware of your surroundings.

Do you frequently compare yourself to others, thinking, "He's so much more talented than I am"?

Do you find yourself comparing your achievements to others? If that's the case, it's essential to avoid comparisons that can lead to feelings of inadequacy. While it's natural to compare ourselves as social beings, it can become detrimental when you compare yourself to a multitude of people, each possessing a desirable attribute. For instance, aspiring to have the body of an Olympian, the intelligence of a mathematician, and the success of a business tycoon all at once is unrealistic. These individuals devote their lives to their crafts, so stop comparing yourself to the unattainable and focus on your unique journey.

Do you set unrealistically high expectations for yourself and feel disheartened when you don't meet them?

If you set impossible standards of perfection, it's crucial to be realistic about what you can achieve given your current level of experience and knowledge. While goals and aspirations are important, setting unattainable standards can lead to disappointment and failure.

Do you find yourself fixating on tasks you believe you should be completing, such as exercising more, speaking up in meetings, or working harder?

If your self-talk dictates how you 'should' live your life, reframe those thoughts by turning 'should' into 'could'. The term 'should' implies obligation, which can feel restrictive. In contrast, 'could' suggests choice and possibility, making it sound more motivating and empowering. For instance, "I could attend more networking events" feels more inviting than "I should attend more networking events."

Do you tend to magnify your perceived shortcomings, thinking, "I always stumble over my words in presentations"?

If you tend to exaggerate your flaws, avoid over-generalising. It's easy to slip into thinking patterns that suggest you're always awkward in social situations or never good at initiating conversations. Instead, examine the reality of these situations: you may find that your negative self-talk is based on a single experience rather than a consistent pattern.

Do you blow minor setbacks out of proportion, telling yourself "This mistake could cost me my job"?

If you tend to blow things out of proportion, take a step back and recognise that you might be overreacting. Ask yourself if the situation is truly as significant as it seems. Try to be more objective—what would you tell your best friend if they were in your shoes? How would you help them put the situation into perspective?

By questioning your self-talk in these ways, you can break free from negative thought patterns and cultivate a mindset that fosters resilience, confidence, and self-compassion. If this alone isn't enough to shift your self-talk, the next step is to challenge your Meta Model patterns. Let's begin by exploring how to challenge generalisations.

10.02 Challenging Generalisations

The core of this process involves asking very specific, probing questions that help you reconnect your generalised thinking (expressed as your self-talk) with the objective truth, clearing away the mental noise and exaggerations that may have clouded your judgement. When you challenge these filters, you essentially start to strip away the assumptions and biases that have been unconsciously influencing your behaviour. This process enables you to examine situations with greater clarity and accuracy, uncovering the real facts instead of being swayed by distorted perceptions. By doing so, you empower yourself to take more informed and effective action, rather than reacting based on incomplete or exaggerated thoughts. Let's start with how to challenge Modal Operator of Necessity.

Modal Operator of Necessity

As you learned in section 9.05, Modal Operator of Necessity are statements that impose rigid, absolute rules on how we *must*, *should*, or *have to* behave. They often create unnecessary pressure, leaving little room for flexibility or personal choice. When we operate under these strict mental rules, we can feel overwhelmed, anxious, or even paralysed by unrealistic expectations.

The key to overcoming this pattern is to challenge these rigid statements by shifting your language from obligation to possibility. Instead of treating these rules as absolute truths, introduce choice and flexibility into your thinking by questioning them.

For example, imagine you catch yourself saying, *"I must reply to all my emails before the end of the day."* A useful way to challenge this thought is by asking, *"What would happen if I didn't?"* By considering the actual consequences, you might realise that delaying some responses until tomorrow wouldn't be catastrophic—it might even be a smarter use of your time.

Or suppose you think, *"I shouldn't take a break right now."* Ask yourself, *"Who says I shouldn't?"* Examining the source of this thought helps you determine whether it's truly valid. Are you genuinely under a deadline, or are you following an unnecessary, self-imposed rule? When you pause to evaluate, you may realise that a short break could actually boost your productivity.

By challenging Modal Operator of Necessity, you free yourself from self-imposed restrictions and gain the power to make choices that align with your needs, goals, and well-being.

Modal Operator of Possibility

Modal Operator of Possibility shape the way we perceive what is or isn't achievable. When we use restrictive language like *"I can't," "It's impossible,"* or *"I'll never,"* we unconsciously shut down opportunities before even exploring them. These statements act as mental roadblocks, reinforcing self-doubt and limiting our potential.

The key to challenging this type of thought is to shift the focus from what *isn't* possible to *how it could become* possible. This starts with awareness—recognising when you're using restrictive language—and then actively challenging it to encourage action and solutions.

For example, if you find yourself thinking, *"I can't speak in front of more than two people,"* challenge this belief by asking, *"What would happen if I could?"* This simple question shifts your perspective, opening the door to possibility rather than reinforcing fear.

Or suppose you say, *"It's impossible to get promoted."* Instead of accepting this as fact, ask yourself, *"What would make it possible?"* This changes your mindset from one of limitation to one of strategy, encouraging you to explore steps that could lead to your goal.

Even statements like *"I won't be able to do this"* can be challenged with, *"What would happen if I could?"* Instead of feeling stuck, you begin thinking about solutions and new ways forward.

By challenging Modal Operator of Possibility, you move away from thoughts that create restrictions and turn them into opportunities. You take control of your actions and decisions rather than feeling overwhelmed by perceived limitations.

Universal Quantifiers

Universal Quantifiers include words like 'always', 'never', 'everything', and 'nobody'—words that create extreme, all-or-nothing thinking. When you use these words in your self-talk, you reinforce rigid thinking, making it feel like things will *always* go wrong or *never* improve. This type of thinking can lead to feelings of helplessness and frustration.

The key to breaking free from these absolutes is to challenge them by looking for exceptions. By doing so, you remind yourself that life is rarely black and white, and that setbacks or disappointments are not constants.

For example, if you catch yourself saying, *"This always happens to me,"* challenge this by asking, *"Has there ever been a time when it didn't?"* This simple question forces you to acknowledge moments when things went differently, helping to break the illusion of inevitability.

Similarly, if you think, *"Everything has gone wrong,"* counter this by asking, *"Is there anything that hasn't gone wrong?"* Shifting your focus to even the smallest positive exceptions helps prevent a spiral of negativity.

Or if you tell yourself, *"I never get picked,"* question this assumption with, *"Has there ever been a time when I was picked?"* This forces you to find examples that contradict your blanket statement, breaking the cycle of limiting thoughts.

By challenging Universal Quantifiers, you shift from vague, negative generalisations to more nuanced and realistic thinking. This fosters resilience, a more balanced outlook, and a greater sense of control over your experiences.

Now let's move onto challenging deletions.

10.03 Challenging Deletions

As I introduce in section 9.06, deletions are mental shortcuts that can leave you feeling stuck and disheartened because your mind is unconsciously *deleting* key information—information that, if acknowledged rather than deleted, could shift your perspective and boost your resilience.

Simple Deletion

Simple Deletion is a statement that is vague and lack the specifics needed to fully understand a situation.

For instance, if you find yourself saying, "This is frustrating," you're making a general statement without clarifying what's causing your frustration. This ambiguity can leave you feeling stuck and unsure of how to address the situation. Instead, ask yourself, "What specifically is frustrating me?" This encourages you to identify the root of the issue, enabling you to tackle it more effectively.

Likewise, if you catch yourself thinking, "I'm not good at this," challenge that by asking, "What exactly am I not good at?" Instead of dwelling on a vague sense of inadequacy, this question allows you to identify the specific skills or areas where you feel challenged, giving you a clearer path for improvement.

Or if you think, "I have to figure this out," prompt yourself with questions like, "What exactly do I have to figure out?" This approach helps you break down overwhelming thoughts into manageable actions, strengthening your resilience and your ability to take meaningful action.

Unspecified Verbs

When faced with vague statements in your self-talk, it's crucial to challenge the Unspecified Verbs that can cloud your understanding and hinder your progress. To gain clarity and insight, ask probing questions that prompt you to define your experiences more precisely. For instance, if you say, "She disappointed me," consider asking yourself, "How specifically did she disappoint me?" This helps you identify the specific actions or words that led to your feelings, allowing you to address them directly.

Similarly, if you think, "I didn't do well," challenge this by asking, "What exactly didn't go well?" This encourages you to reflect on the specific aspects of the situation that may need improvement rather than accepting a vague sense of failure.

Or, if you tell yourself, "I made a poor choice," ask, "What specifically made it a poor choice?" This inquiry leads you to analyse the details of your decision, providing insight that can guide you in future situations.

By transforming ambiguous, self-limiting thoughts into clear, constructive statements, you promote problem-solving and enhance your emotional resilience.

Comparative Deletion

When you make comparisons without specifying the context or criteria, you risk undermining your self-esteem and perspective. To challenge these comparisons effectively, ask questions that uncover the unspecified benchmarks and reveal the underlying assumptions.

For instance, if you find yourself thinking, "He's more successful than I am," take a moment to ask, "More successful in what way?" This question prompts you to define the aspects of success you're considering, whether it's career achievements, financial status, or personal fulfilment. By specifying the criteria for success, you can better understand your own accomplishments and set realistic goals.

Similarly, if you say, "This task is more challenging," consider asking yourself, "Challenging in what way, specifically?" This encourages you to examine the specific difficulties you face, whether they stem from a lack of knowledge, skills, or resources. By identifying the precise nature of the challenge, you can develop targeted strategies to address it.

Or, if you think, "I performed poorly in that meeting," challenge this thought by asking, "According to whose standards?" This question helps you reflect on whether your assessment is based on objective criteria, personal expectations, or comparisons to others. By questioning the source of your evaluation, you empower yourself to adopt a more balanced and realistic view of your performance.

By challenging Comparative Deletion, you can turn vague and disempowering thoughts into clear, constructive, and empowering statements that foster personal growth and resilience.

Now let's turn our attention to the final set of Meta Model patterns: Distortions.

10.04 Challenging Distortions

Distorted thoughts can feel incredibly convincing in the moment, leading you to assume that your reality is set in stone. By applying critical questioning skills, however, you'll be able to see situations with greater clarity and accuracy, ultimately strengthening your resilience in the face of life's challenges.

Mind Reading

As you learned in section 9.07, Mind Reading is a common cognitive distortion that occurs when we make assumptions about others' thoughts, feelings, or intentions without any concrete evidence. This type of distortion can lead to unnecessary worry and anxiety, as we often jump to conclusions based on limited information. To effectively challenge Mind Reading, it's essential to ask questions that explore the validity of these assumptions and bring you back to reality.

For instance, if you catch yourself thinking, "They're judging me," pause and ask yourself "How do I know that they're judging me?" Reflect on their expressions and body language—what concrete evidence do you have to support this belief? Often, you might realise that your perception is influenced by your own insecurities or past experiences, rather than any definitive indication from others.

Similarly, if you think, "My boss thinks I'm incompetent," challenge this assumption by asking "How do I know my boss thinks I'm incompetent?" Consider their feedback and interactions with you. Have they directly expressed dissatisfaction, or could this be a misunderstanding based on your self-doubt?

Another example could be, "My friends are annoyed with me." In this case, ask yourself "How do I know that my friends are annoyed with me?" Examine their recent interactions—have they said or done anything to indicate this, or is it possible you're interpreting their behaviour through your own fears or worries about your relationship with them?

By questioning these distorted thoughts, you can replace unfounded assumptions with a more accurate understanding of reality, significantly reducing unnecessary anxiety and emotional turmoil. This process not only enhances your resilience but also fosters healthier relationships with others by promoting clearer communication and understanding.

Nominalisation

To effectively challenge this Meta Model pattern, it's essential to convert abstract nouns into actionable processes (captured as verbs) through targeted questioning. This shift in perspective allows you to move from vague feelings or situations towards a clearer understanding of the specific actions, behaviours, or factors at play.

For instance, if you find yourself thinking, "My behaviour is poor," you can challenge this by asking, "How am I behaving poorly?" This question prompts you to identify the specific actions or patterns in your behaviour that need to be addressed, enabling you to focus on making meaningful changes.

Another common Nominalisation is, "I have anxiety." Instead of accepting this as a fixed state, you can inquire, "What is causing me to feel anxious?" This question encourages you to explore the underlying triggers and circumstances contributing to your anxiety, empowering you to take proactive steps toward managing it.

Similarly, if you express the thought, "The decision I've made is terrible," challenge it by asking, "How am I deciding terribly?" This prompts you to reflect on the decision-making process and the factors influencing your judgement, allowing you to clarify your reasoning and potentially revise your decision.

By challenging Nominalisation in this way, you transform your self-talk from a static, fixed perspective into a dynamic process. Use this approach to identify actionable steps and create opportunities for improvement or change, through which you can foster a more constructive mindset.

Cause-Effect

To effectively challenge Cause-Effect thinking, it's important to identify phrases that imply a direct causal relationship between two events or feelings. Common phrases include 'makes me', 'because of', and 'leads to'. By asking clarifying questions, you can investigate these automatic connections more deeply. For instance, consider asking, "How specifically does this cause that?" This approach helps to unravel the assumptions behind these connections and encourages more flexible thinking.

For example, if you find yourself thinking, "The noise from my neighbours makes me anxious," you can challenge this by asking, "What specifically do they do that causes me to feel anxious?" This encourages you to reflect on your response to the noise and consider other factors that might contribute to your feelings of anxiety.

Another common thought might be, "I can't pursue my dreams because of my lack of experience." You can question this by asking, "What is it about my lack of experience that leads me to think I can't pursue my dreams?" This prompts you to examine your assumptions about experience and success, and changes your perspective.

Similarly, you may think, "If I ask for help, people will think I'm weak." To challenge this assumption, ask, "How will asking for help cause people to think I'm weak?" This not only questions the connection between cause and effect, but also opens up the possibility that asking for help might actually be seen as a sign of strength.

When you challenge Cause-Effect thinking in this way, you can reveal the assumptions that underpin perceived connections and explore alternative perspectives. You can then respond more resiliently to situations, and take action based on a clearer understanding of your thoughts.

Complex Equivalence

These Meta Model patterns occur when you equate one thing with another without sufficient evidence, assuming a direct relationship between the two. This can often lead to a rigid interpretation of events, leaving little room for alternative explanations. To effectively challenge Complex Equivalence, it's essential to question the assumed connections by asking, "How does this mean that?" This approach will open your mind to explore other possible meanings and interpretations, fostering a more flexible and resilient mindset.

For example, consider the thought, "My friend didn't reply to my message. They must be upset with me." To challenge this assumption, ask yourself, "How does their not replying mean that they are upset with me?" This encourages you to consider other possibilities, such as the friend being busy or preoccupied, rather than jumping to conclusions about their feelings.

Another instance might be, "I made a mistake during the presentation. My colleagues think I'm incompetent." Here, you can challenge the connection by asking, "How does making a mistake mean that my colleagues think I'm incompetent?" This question prompts you to recognise that mistakes are a natural part of learning and do not define your overall competence.

Similarly, if you find yourself thinking, "I forgot to go to the meeting. My boss will fire me because of this." You can ask, "How does forgetting to go to the meeting mean my boss will fire me?" This opens the door to realising that one mistake does not necessarily lead to such a drastic conclusion and that your boss may understand and forgive the oversight.

By questioning Complex Equivalence in this way, you can move away from fixed mindsets towards more adaptable perspectives, enabling you to navigate life's challenges with greater resilience and understanding.

You now have all the information you need to challenge your own mental shortcuts. The best way to make use of that information is to practice, practice, practice. Let's do that next.

Activity 18: Question the Thinking Traps!

In Activity 16 in the previous chapter , you identified which Meta Model pattern corresponded to each type of self-talk I'd introduced. Now it's your opportunity to challenge these thoughts! (Once you've completed the activity, you'll find the correct answers and explanations below.)

1. **"I'm such an idiot."** → Complex Equivalence
    - Challenge question:

2. **"He's so much more talented than I am."** → Comparative Deletion
    - Challenge question:

3. **"I must always meet my own high standards."** → Modal Operator of Necessity
    - Challenge question:

4. **"They probably think I'm lazy."** → Mind Reading
    - Challenge question:

5. **"I always stumble over my words in presentations."** → Universal Quantifier
    - Challenge question:

6. "This mistake could cost me my job." → Cause-Effect

- Challenge question:

Spoiler Alert: Here are the answers for Activity 18

1. "I'm such an idiot." → Complex Equivalence

- Challenge question: "How does what's happened mean I'm an idiot?"

2. "He's so much more talented than I am." → Comparative Deletion

- Challenge question: "How specifically is he more talented than me? Who says? According to whose standards?"

3. "I must always meet my own high standards." → Modal Operator of Necessity

- Challenge question: "What would happen if I didn't meet my own high standards?"

- Challenge question: (Bonus points if you noticed the Universal Quantifier—*always*—here too.) "Always? Has there ever been a time when I didn't meet my own high standards?"

4. "They probably think I'm lazy." → Mind Reading

- Challenge question: "Who says I should? According to whom? What would happen if I didn't?"

5. "I always stumble over my words in presentations." → Universal Quantifier

- Challenge question: "Always? Has there ever been a time when I haven't stumbled over my words in a presentation?"

6. "This mistake could cost me my job." → Cause-Effect

- Challenge question: "How is this mistake going to cost me my job?"

Here are some more questions to practice your challenging of mental shortcuts.

Activity 19: Generic Meta Model Quiz

The following sentences are mixed up. Your task is to:

    i. Name the type of mental shortcut.

    ii. Think of a question that would challenge it.

1. It's important. →
2. His communication is poor. →
3. I handled that badly. →
4. She's better than me. →
5. It's impossible to find a job I enjoy. →
6. They make me feel unimportant. →
7. I should always be productive. →
8. Nobody ever listens to me. →
9. I feel uncomfortable. →
10. I must never make mistakes. →
11. They don't like me. →
12. I have to be perfect at this. →
13. I can't learn new skills at my age. →
14. I stumbled over my words, which means I'm terrible at public speaking. →
15. I did that badly. →
16. I'll never be able to run a marathon. →
17. I always get overlooked. →
18. The fear is overwhelming. . →
19. He thinks I'm an idiot. →

20. He hurt me. →

21. She disagreed with me, so she must not respect my opinion. →

22. I can't succeed because of my past. →

23. Everything I do goes wrong. →

24. I need to do this. →

25. I created a bad impression on them. →

26. That is easier. →

27. She wishes I wasn't working on this project. →

28. The stress is too much. →

29. If I fail, everyone will think I'm useless. →

30. He didn't say thank you, so he must not appreciate me. →

Spoiler Alert: Here are the answers for Activity 19

1. It's important. → Simple Deletion → *What exactly is important?*

2. His communication is poor. → Nominalisation → *How is he communicating poorly?*

3. I handled that badly. → Unspecified Verb → *What specifically did I handle badly? What specifically did I do that caused me to think that I handled that badly?*

4. She's better than me. → Comparative Deletion → *How specifically is she better than me? In what context? According to whom?*

5. It's impossible to find a job I enjoy. → Modal Operator of Possibility → *What would make it possible?*

6. They make me feel unimportant. → Cause-Effect → *What specifically do they do that causes me to feel unimportant?*

7. I should always be productive. → Modal Operator of Necessity → *Who says?*

8. Nobody ever listens to me. → Universal Quantifier → *Nobody? Is there anyone who does listen to me?*

9. I feel uncomfortable. → Simple Deletion → *What specifically am I uncomfortable about?*

10. I must never make mistakes. → Modal Operator of Necessity → *What would happen if I did?*

11. They don't like me. → Mind Reading → *How do I know that they don't like me? What specific actions or words lead me to believe this?*

12. I have to be perfect at this. → Modal Operator of Necessity → *What if I didn't have to be perfect?*

13. I can't learn new skills at my age. → Modal Operator of Possibility → *Who says? What if I could?*

14. I stumbled over my words, which means I'm terrible at public speaking. → Complex Equivalence → *How does stumbling over my words mean I'm terrible at public speaking?*

15. I did that badly. → Comparative Deletion → *Compared to what—or whose—standard did I do badly?*

16. I'll never be able to run a marathon. → Modal Operator of Possibility → *Who says? What would happen if I could?*

17. I always get overlooked. → Universal Quantifier → *Always? Has there ever been a time when I haven't been overlooked?*

18. The fear is overwhelming. → Nominalisation → *What specifically do I fear that's overwhelming me?*

19. He thinks I'm an idiot. → Mind Reading → *How do I know that he thinks I'm an idiot? What has he said or done to suggest this?*

20. He hurt me. → Unspecified Verb → *How specifically did he hurt me? What specifically did he do that caused me to feel hurt?*

21. She disagreed with me, so she must not respect my opinion. → Complex Equivalence → *How does her disagreeing with me mean she doesn't respect my opinion?*

22. I can't succeed because of my past. → Cause-Effect → *What is it about my past that causes me to think I can't succeed?*

23. Everything I do goes wrong. → Universal Quantifier → *Everything? Is there anything I've done that hasn't gone wrong?*

24. I need to do this. → Simple Deletion → *What exactly do I need to do? By when? Why?*

25. I created a bad impression on them. → Unspecified Verb → *In what way specifically did I create a bad impression on them?*

26. That is easier. → Comparative Deletion → *Easier than what? For whom is it easier?*

27. She wishes I wasn't working on this project. → Mind Reading → *How do I know that she feels this way? What evidence supports this assumption?*

28. The stress is too much. → Nominalisation → *What is stressing me too much?*

29. If I fail, everyone will think I'm useless. → Cause-Effect → *How will failing cause everyone to think I'm useless?*

30. He didn't say thank you, so he must not appreciate me. → Complex Equivalence → *How does him not saying thank you mean he doesn't appreciate me?*

Activity 20: Identifying Your Meta Model Patterns

Now that you have some practice under your belt, it's time to explore the Meta Model patterns in your own self-talk and objectives. This activity will help you recognise the mental shortcuts that may be holding you back and will empower you to challenge them.

Steps to Complete the Activity:

1. **Refer to Your Objectives:** Go back to the objectives you identified in Activity 17 in the previous chapter. Think about the self-talk and mental shortcuts that were holding you back from achieving those objectives.

2. **Challenge Your Thoughts:** Having identified the mental shortcuts that are leading to your self-talk, ask yourself one or more Meta Model questions. This will help to loosen your thinking, gain a new perspective, and turn your Success Cycle in a positive direction that enhances your resilience.

3. **Reflect on What You've Learned:** Take some time to consider what insights you gained from this process. What new perspectives have you uncovered about your objectives and the self-talk that accompanies them?

4. **Identify Action Steps:** Based on your reflections, jot down specific actions you can take moving forward to help to achieve your objectives.

Example - Sam's Answer:

To illustrate how this process works, here's an example featuring Sam:

Objective: I want to be able to switch off from work.

- **Self-Talk:** "I must keep on top of my workload."
- **Shortcut Identified:** Modal Operator of Necessity
- **Meta Model Challenge:** What will happen if I don't keep on top of my workload?
- **Answer:** I'll worry that I'll fall behind and Belle will think I'm incapable.

Answer contains a second shortcut: Complex Equivalence

- **Meta Model Challenge:** How will falling behind mean that Belle will think I'm incapable?
- **Answer:** It doesn't!

Objective: I want to let go and move on when things don't go well.

- **Self-Talk:** "How have I messed up?"
- **Shortcut Identified:** Complex Equivalence
- **Meta Model Challenge:** How does something not going well mean I've messed up?
- **Answer:** I guess it doesn't!

Objective: I want to feel comfortable delivering last-minute presentations.

- **Self-Talk:** "I'm scared of everyone judging me."
- **Shortcuts Identified:**
    1. Universal Quantifier
    2. Unspecified Verb
    3. Complex Equivalence
- **Meta Model Challenge to shortcut 1:** Who is 'everyone'?
- **Answer:** The whole team.

(As that didn't work, let's try a different question.)

- **Meta Model Challenge to shortcut 2:** How will everyone judge me?
- **Answer:** They all wish Belle was doing the presentation; she's so much better than me.

Answer contains a second shortcut: Comparative Deletion

- **Meta Model Challenge:** How specifically is Belle better than me?
- **Answer:** Belle is much more confident, authoritative, knowledgeable, and articulate than I am. That's why they all wish she were doing the presentation instead of me.

Answer contains a third shortcut: Mind Reading

- **Meta Model Challenge:** How do I know that they all wish Belle was doing this?
- **Answer:** I can't answer this! I've made an assumption, haven't I? This process of questioning has made me realise that I am hard on myself. I expect to be as good as Belle, who has been working for a lot longer than I have! I feel marginally better now.
- **Meta Model Challenge to shortcut 3:** How does giving last-minute presentations mean I'll be judged?
- **Answer:** Because if I can't answer their questions, they'll think I'm incompetent or not good enough.

Answer contains a second shortcut: Complex Equivalence

- **Meta Model Challenge:** How does not being able to answer their questions mean that they'll think I'm incompetent or not good enough? (There's also an example of Mind Reading here: How do I know that they'll think this?!)
- **Answer:** I guess it doesn't!

Sam's Reflections:

"Going through this process has been quite eye-opening for me. I realised that I've been putting a tremendous amount of pressure on my shoulders by comparing myself to Belle. I

hadn't fully understood how much I internalised the idea that I needed to match her level of competence, which is ridiculous: she's been doing this job for far longer than I have! Recognising the irrationality of that thinking is liberating, but it's also disheartening to see a recurring theme in my self-talk: the assumption that I'm incapable, incompetent, or simply not good enough. It's challenging to confront those feelings, but I recognise that these assumptions are barriers to my growth and well-being.

In terms of specific actions I can take moving forward, I will pay attention to my self-talk and be mindful to challenge it when I notice a deletion, distortion or generalisation."

If, like Sam, you find some of these realisations uncomfortable, don't worry! This is just the beginning. You're about to learn more about yourself, including the underlying reasons for your automatic thoughts, feelings, and behaviours.

Chapter Summary

As your self-talk will be a constant in your life, you need to ensure it's your best friend, not your enemy. If your thoughts are working against you, remember that it's only because System 1 is operating in default mode. Once you realise this, the first step in changing the voice inside your head is to be aware of what it is saying. You can then consciously change that voice by engaging System 2 and challenging the deletions, distortions, and generalisations in your thoughts and self-talk.

Be mindful that these mental patterns often present themselves as undeniable truths because System 1 operates automatically in the background, shaping your perception of reality without conscious examination. Before you became aware of these cognitive shortcuts, you likely accepted them as facts, oblivious to the reality that they stemmed from your personal experiences and biases. However, by engaging System 2, you can illuminate these hidden filters, question their accuracy, and reveal a clearer perspective. With time and practice, this transformation will enhance your ability to approach challenges with improved clarity, resilience, and confidence.

What's Next?

By examining each element of The Success Cycle, you now understand how to override System 1's default mode and consciously change your behaviour, feelings, and thoughts. This will enable you to appear more confident, be more assertive, feel more courageous, and think in a more resilient way. Hopefully, you have employed the tools and techniques that resonate with you and have already noticed significant shifts.

While you have completed Part Two, your overall journey has not yet finished. There may still be certain areas in your professional life that leave you feeling miserable or that prevent you from achieving the results you desire, no matter how many times you put the techniques featured in this book into practice.

As you discovered in Part One, it is not possible to change all your limitations in the ways set out during Part 2. In some instances, System 1's default mode of operation is too ingrained to be overridden by System 2 alone; it needs to be reprogrammed. You'll learn how in Part Three.

PART THREE:
REPROGRAMMING YOUR MIND FOR UNSHAKEABLE SELF-BELIEF

Congratulations! If you've been following the steps outlined in this book so far, you are already on your way to steering your Success Cycle in a positive direction. You have gained numerous self-coaching techniques to consciously engage System 2 and override the automatic responses of System 1, helping you to build confidence, courage, and resilience.

While these strategies can create powerful, immediate changes, true and lasting growth requires you to address the root causes of your automatic behaviours. In Part Three, you'll explore the hidden programming within your mind—the unconscious forces shaping your confidence, courage, and resilience in ways you may not yet recognise. You'll discover what this programming is, how it drives your Success Cycle by influencing your perception of yourself and the world around you.

Most importantly, you'll learn how to use self-coaching techniques to identify, disrupt, and rewrite these ingrained patterns, ensuring they no longer dictate your actions. By rewiring System 1, you'll move beyond the need to consciously override automatic responses. Instead, confidence, courage, and resilience will become your natural state, empowering you to break free from self-sabotage and embrace a new reality where you thrive in every situation.

If you're wondering why we focused first on engaging System 2 to *override* System 1 instead of jumping straight *rewiring* it, it's because Part One and Part Two laid the essential groundwork. You've already done much of the heavy lifting! Now, you're fully prepared to apply what comes next.

THE INNER MECHANICS OF
LASTING CONFIDENCE

"What is real? If real is what you can feel, smell, taste and see, then 'real' is simply electrical signals interpreted by your brain."
Morpheus[47]

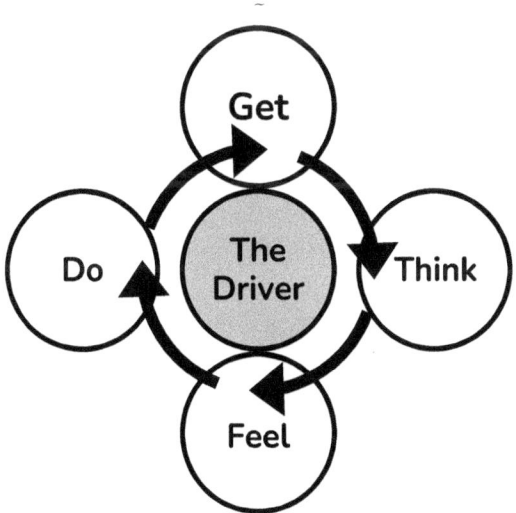

Sam has made a consistent effort to put the techniques she has learned into practice. As a result, she feels she has made significant progress towards many of her objectives. She now consciously makes more eye contact in meetings, pauses more

---

[47] *Morpheus is one of the central characters in the 1999 iconic film, The Matrix*

often when speaking, and engages in non-work-related chats with colleagues whenever she has time. If she's busy, she politely but firmly suggests catching up over lunch instead.

She has also been practicing taking pauses whenever she catches herself about to say 'um', 'er', or another filler word. At home, she no longer snaps at Davide over minor irritations. In fact, if she ever feels on the verge of lashing out, she stops herself and instead gets curious about the real source of her frustration. She reflects on her day at work and considers whether she may have been too passive in a situation. This self-awareness helps her plan how to be more assertive if a similar scenario arises in the future.

Her relationship with Belle has completely transformed. She now understands that when Belle asks her to take on a last-minute presentation, it's not to burden her: it's an opportunity to help her grow in her career. Likewise, the dynamic between Sam and Muhammed has changed for the better: he's now surprisingly supportive!

Yet despite her progress, Sam still struggles with self-promotion and stepping outside of her comfort zone. While she no longer dreads delivering last-minute presentations, they still make her feel uncomfortable. She also finds it difficult to switch off from work and let go when things don't go as planned. Most frustratingly, she still feels no closer to achieving her ultimate goal: becoming Project Manager.

If you're like Sam—making steady improvements yet still grappling with persistent challenges—don't worry. No matter how many times you've used the techniques in this book, some patterns run so deep that they require more than conscious effort to change.

So far, we've focused on using System 2—your conscious, rational thinking—to override System 1, your brain's automatic default mode. But as you learned in *The Mind Quiz (Chapter 1)*, System 1 is sometimes so confident in its response that it doesn't even realise it needs System 2's help: there's no opportunity for you to force System 2 to intervene. Instead, you need to reprogramme System 1 itself.

In this chapter, you'll uncover why System 1 needs reprogramming and how its ingrained patterns shape your reality. Then, in the next chapter, you'll learn how to rewire System 1 so that confidence, assertiveness, courage and resilience become your new default settings.

What This Chapter Covers:

- 11.01 Hidden Programming
- 11.02 How Programmes Shape Reality
- 11.03 Reality Quiz
- 11.04 Unveiling Reality: Answers to the Reality Quiz
- 11.05 What the Quiz Reveals About Your Reality
- 11.06 When Programmes Fail You
- 11.07 What the Programmes Are
- 11.08 How Change is Possible

11.01 Hidden Programming

In Chapter 2, you learned that a set of instructions—called *programmes*—are embedded in System 1 by the time you turn seven. This happens because the survival of our ancestors depended on them working together in a world filled with danger—especially in harsh, predator-filled environments. As a result, humans evolved as social animals, relying on cooperation to stay alive. This ingrained in us an innate desire to fit in and belong. After all, being shunned from the group often meant certain death.

To be part of a group, it became essential to adopt the rules by which that group lived. These rules still exist today. From the moment you are born, you are programmed with a set of rules that help you survive and integrate into your society.

These rules form your programming, which in turn shapes your ethics, expectations, and attitudes. You are taught about gender roles, social class, religion, and ethnicity—how you identify within these categories and what that means for you. For example, if you are raised in Western societies, you might learn that success means getting an education, securing a job, buying a home, and starting a family (not necessarily in that order). You might also be taught that external achievements—such as love, wealth, and material possessions—lead to happiness. Additionally, you may learn that beauty is defined by physical appearance and that authority figures, such as teachers, politicians, doctors, and police officers, should be trusted and obeyed. These messages are conveyed explicitly and implicitly through the media, education, peers, family and colleagues.

It's important to recognise that your *programmes* are neither universally 'right' nor 'wrong'. They simply help you to navigate your specific environment. These deeply embedded scripts are what run System 1. They influence your thoughts, feelings, and behaviours through the Success Cycle, ultimately determining your levels of confidence, courage, and resilience.

While System 1 and System 2 are *designed* to work together seamlessly, the reality is obviously different. If it weren't, self-sabotage wouldn't occur. To understand what actually happens, we must turn our focus to the mind and the nature of reality.

11.02 How Programmes Shape Reality

Your brain is encased in a dark, silent place: your skull. Here, it is completely disconnected from the outside world: it never experiences the external world directly. Instead, it relies on your five senses—sight, sound, smell, touch, and taste—to gather information. This presents a unique challenge: while your sensory systems are remarkable, they are also biologically limited. As a result, your perception of reality is incomplete and filtered.

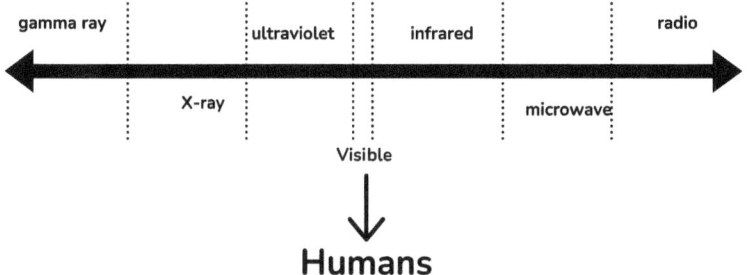

Take vision, for example. The electromagnetic spectrum consists of electromagnetic radiation that spans a vast range of frequencies, from low to high. However, our eyes detect only a tiny fraction of this spectrum—known as visible light. To put this into perspective, we perceive just one ten-trillionth of the electromagnetic spectrum, while other species experience the electromagnetic spectrum differently. Insects, for instance, can see ultraviolet light, which makes flowers appear entirely different to them than they do to us. In other words, what you see as reality may be perceived entirely differently by another species.

The same is true for hearing. Our hearing has an upper limit of around 20 kHz, whereas a dog's hearing extends up 45 kHz. This is why a dog whistle, which emits frequencies between 23 to 54 kHz, is silent to us but perfectly audible to dogs. The diagram below illustrates the frequency ranges perceived by humans and some common mammals. Sounds below 20 Hz are classified as infrasounds—detectable by animals such as elephants—while sounds above 20 kHz are ultrasounds, perceived by species like dogs (up to 50 kHz) and bats (up to 120 kHz).

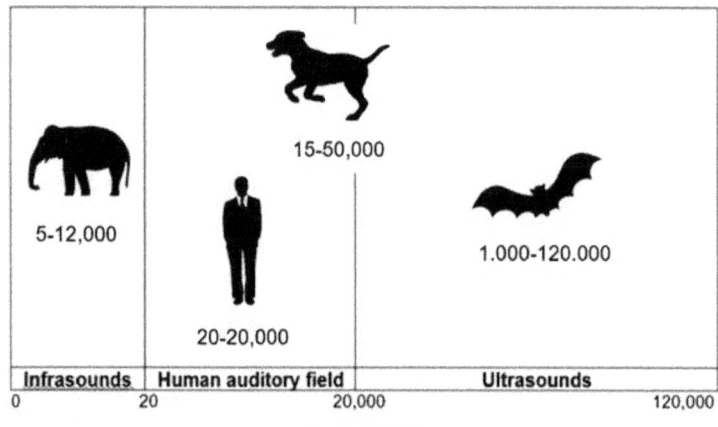

Stranger still, things like colour, sound, and smell don't actually exist in the world. Your sensory organs detect photons of light, air compression waves, and chemical molecules, then convert them into electrochemical signals that your brain interprets as colour, sound, and smell.

According to Dr. Mazviita Chirimuuta, author of *Outside Color: Perceptual Science and the Puzzle of Color in Philosophy*, colour is an illusion. She explains that only light exists, and your brain transforms that light into the experience of colour. In other words:

- Colours don't exist outside of your brain: your mind creates them.
- Sounds aren't 'real': they're simply your brain's interpretation of vibrations.
- Smells are just chemical signals that your brain translates into a sensory experience.

In summary, everything you experience as reality is not a direct encounter with the world but 'an electrochemical rendition in a dark theatre'.[48] So, can you truly trust what you see as real?

By now, you know the answer is 'no'.

---

[48] Eagleman, D. (2015). *The Brain*. Canongate Books Ltd.

Even though you see, hear, feel, smell, and taste, what you perceive as reality is simply your brain's interpretation of the world. And what influences this interpretation? Your programmes. Your brain filters external information through these programmes to generate your *internal reality*. This, in turn, becomes your *external reality* (how you experience the world).

It does this using the three unconscious mechanisms we first encountered in Chapter 3:

- Deletion: Ignoring certain details.
- Distortion: Altering information to fit pre-existing assumptions.
- Generalisation: Applying specific experiences broadly.

These filters shape how you perceive and respond to the world—without you even realising it.

In essence, your brain is an incredible machine, working tirelessly to make sense of the world around you so you can survive and thrive. But it doesn't process reality as it actually is—it filters, shortcuts, and sometimes even alters information to fit what it expects to see.

11.03 Reality Quiz

To understand just how much of your reality is shaped by your brain's unconscious processing, complete the following activity. You'll experience firsthand how your mind fills in gaps, ignores details, and even changes what you perceive—all to save time and energy.

Activity 21a: Scrambled Words

Can you read the following paragraph:

> Yuor biran is amzanig. Trehe are no two wyas auobt it. Insaetd of rbuieldnig yuor ralitey form satcrch eevry memnot, it campores icnomnig sesonry dtaa wtih a moedel taht it has alradey cnostrctued.

Activity 21b: Invisible Words

Read the text in this triangle:

What does it say?

 Activity 21c: How Many Fs?

Read the following text while counting how many Fs there are:

> FINISHED FILES ARE THE RE
> SULT OF YEARS OF SCIENTI
> FIC STUDY COMBINED WITH
> THE EXPERIENCE OF YEARS...

How many Fs do you count?

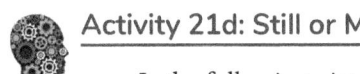

Activity 21d: Still or Moving?

Is the following picture still or is it moving?

11.04 Unveiling Reality: Answers to the Reality Quiz

Let's find out how you got on, and what these illusions reveal about the nature of reality.

21a Scrambled Words

How much of the gobbledegook could you read?

Probably most of it! Your brain doesn't rely on every single letter: it recognises patterns and fills in the gaps based on what it expects. So even though the letters are mixed up, your brain automatically corrects them. This is an example of generalisation, where your mind assumes meaning based on prior experience.

Here's the translation of the gobbledegook:

Your brain is amazing. There are no two ways about it. Instead of rebuilding your reality from scratch every moment, it compares incoming sensory data with a model that it has already constructed.

Researchers think that the order of most letters in a word doesn't matter: provided that the first and last letter are in the right place, you are still able to read the word, even if the rest of the letters are jumbled up.[49] (There are exceptions, however: we can interpret shorter words more reliably than longer ones.)

21b: The Invisible Double Word

When you read 'A BIRD IN THE THE BUSH', did you spot the repeated 'the'? Most people miss it! Your brain expects only one 'the', so it automatically deletes the extra one—even though it's right there. This is an example of deletion, where your mind filters out what it considers unnecessary. This shows how expectation overrides reality.

Notice that System 1 deletes the second THE outside of your conscious awareness, but as soon as it is pointed out to you, you are able to see both THEs effortlessly. This highlights the process of being able to over-ride System 1's mental shortcuts by engaging System 2, which I explored in Part Two.

21c: Missing Letters

How many F's did you count? Three? There are actually six!

Your brain tends to skip over small, common words like 'OF' because it focuses on the more meaningful ones. This is another form of deletion, where information is ignored without you realising it.

Notice again how you can see all six Fs effortlessly as soon as the illusion has been brought to your conscious awareness. Sometimes, however, System 1's mental shortcuts are so hard-wired that it's not possible to change what you see even when you are aware of the illusion, as the next quiz question demonstrated.

---

[49] Bolton, D. (2016). *The reason why this 'difficult' puzzle is so easy to read*. The Independent. https://www.independent.co.uk/news/science/jumbled-words-letters-puzzle-cambridge-a6889811.html

21d: The Moving Illusion

Since the image is in a book, it is obviously still. Yet, it appears to move, despite the reader knowing that it's a static, printed image. Why? Your brain predicts motion based on past experience, creating an illusion known as Peripheral Drift. This is an example of distortion—where your brain modifies what you see. Researchers believe that the arrangement of light and dark colours in images like this tricks motion-sensitive neurons into responding as if they were perceiving real physical motion.[50]

Interestingly, even though you consciously know the image is static, you cannot engage System 2 to override how System 1 interprets it. This highlights why certain self-sabotaging behaviours cannot be changed simply by engaging System 2 alone, and explains why reprogramming System 1 can be necessary.

These illusions reveal a fundamental truth: what you perceive isn't always real. Your mind filters, distorts, and fills in gaps—all without your awareness. This is why understanding these mental shortcuts is so important.

11.05 What the Quiz Reveals About Your Reality

Your brain isn't maliciously trying to trick you—it's simply working as efficiently as possible to make sense of the world with the information it has. Its primary goal is to help you survive and conserve energy. Most of the time, your brain's interpretation is accurate. As you've seen from these illusions, though, it doesn't always get things right.

In essence, reality—as you experience it—is a projection of what your brain *expects* to see. Your unconscious programmes, embedded in System 1, shape what you notice, how you interpret it, and how you

---

[50] O'Reilly, M.. Understanding the rotating snakes illusion. UCL. www.ucl.ac.uk/~ucbpmor/docs/case_study3_mor_web.pdf

respond, creating a self-fulfilling prophecy that drives the Success Cycle either in your favour or against you.

Your brain doesn't passively absorb the world around you. It actively *constructs* it, unconsciously shaping reality to align with your expectations. In other words, your perception is less about what's *out there* and more about what's already in your head. This leads to a powerful truth:

Your brain sees what it expects to see based on your programmes.

If you feel resistance to this idea—perhaps even arguing with me in your head right now—that's proof of just how deeply ingrained these programmes can be. They feel like absolute truths because they so convincingly shape your experiences.

Let's look at how this plays out in the Success Cycle. If your programming tells you that you can't give a presentation without messing up...

- You think: *"I can't do this. I'll mess up. I'll embarrass myself. People will see right through me."*
- These thoughts create feelings of self-doubt and anxiety.
- Those feelings lead to actions—like avoiding presentations altogether.
- The result? You miss opportunities to practice and prove to yourself that you *can* deliver a presentation. And if you do try, your negative self-talk takes over, leaving no mental space to remember what you're supposed to say.
- You also delete any positive experiences, focusing only on what went wrong. Even if you do a good job and a colleague compliments you afterward, you distort it, thinking, *"They're just being nice."*

- This reinforces the programme that you can't give a presentation without messing up—trapping you in a self-fulfilling cycle.

This example illustrates how your programmes determine what you *pay attention to,* and what you *ignore.* In so doing, they trigger a chain reaction of thoughts, emotions, and behaviours that drive the Success Cycle in the wrong direction.

11.06 When Programmes Fail You

But why do some of our System 1 programmes hold us back, rather than helping us? The root of the issue lies in the fact that much of your brain's programming is formed during childhood.

It is widely thought that we are encoded with many of our programmes by the time we're seven. Sociologist and author of *The People Puzzle,* Morris Massey, described the period up to the age of seven as the *imprint period.*

Massey thought that this imprint period exists because, up to the age of seven, we are like sponges: we absorb everything around us and accept much of what we are told as being true, without question. He proposed that, during the imprint period, a child learns a sense of what is right and wrong, fair and unfair, good and bad. So, if a child learns that their mother gives them milk when they cry, they start to form a programme that the world is safe. When they stagger across a room for the first time, and everyone claps and smiles, they begin to think that they are clever. Every event in their life shapes their view of themselves (their programmes about themselves) and the world around them (their programmes about the world).

Essentially, because a child is unable to critically evaluate or challenge what they are told, it gives trusted sources (parents, guardians, teachers, and other authority figures) unfiltered access to how System 1 is programmed.

For example, 'no' is one of the most common words parents say to their children. While this is necessary for their safety—such as preventing them from putting a finger in an electric socket—it may also unintentionally create a programme that they are inherently wrong. These early messages play a crucial role in shaping how children perceive themselves and the world, leading to programming like *'I am wrong'* or *'My needs don't matter.'*

Consider another example: a global pandemic. Children are told to stay at least a metre away from others, wear masks, and sanitise their hands constantly. Meanwhile, the media bombards them with images of overcrowded hospitals, medical professionals covered head to toe in protective clothing, mass grave sites, and updates on infection rates and deaths. These messages—intentionally or not—could shape a child's perception of the world as a scary and unsafe place. Consequently, some children might develop programmes like *'No matter what I do, I'll struggle'*, *'The world is out to get me'*, or *'Other people are dangerous'*. [51] Conversely, children not exposed to such images might instead develop more optimistic programmes like *'I can look forward to a bright future'*, *'There is always hope'*, or *'I will always be safe'*.

Another challenge with programming being imprinted early in life is that young children are naturally egocentric. Lacking an awareness of perspectives outside their own, they assume that whatever happens around them is their fault. For example, if a child's parents divorce, they may conclude that they caused it. This can lead to programmes like *'I'm bad'*, *'I'm guilty'*, or *'I'm unlovable'*. While these programmes are entirely false, they shape how the child views themselves and responds to the world.

Another problem that can arise is that some programmes may be beneficial in one context but limiting in another.

EXAMPLE: WIN AT ALL COSTS

A programme like *'I must win'* could be highly beneficial for a sports professional or a businessperson striving to

---

[51] Morin, A. (2017). Three important ways your childhood shaped who you are. Psychology Today. https://www.psychologytoday.com/us/blog/what-mentally-strong-people-dont-do/201709/3-important-ways-your-childhood-shaped-who-you-are

reach the top of their field. It's likely that every world champion or successful entrepreneur holds a programme along these lines.

However, this same programme may have negative consequences in other areas of life, particularly relationships. If a major life event occurs, such as retirement or personal loss, a person with this programme might find themselves isolated. They may have neglected meaningful connections along the way, or even damaged relationships by prioritising personal success over others.

Or a programme that helps you survive in childhood may become an obstacle in adulthood.

EXAMPLE: FEAR OF MAKING MISTAKES

A child raised in a highly critical household might adopt the programme that *'Mistakes are unacceptable'*. This could drive them to excel academically and become highly detail-oriented—both beneficial traits in school. However, in the workplace, this same programme may lead to perfectionism, a fear of taking risks, or avoidance of innovative projects during which failure is a possibility. Over time, this could stifle their career growth, creativity, and overall well-being.

The Danger of Unquestioned Obedience

Society also instils powerful, unquestioned programmes, such as the importance of obeying authority.

In 1961, psychologist Stanley Milgram conducted a now-famous experiment to investigate why individuals at the Nuremberg trials claimed they were 'just following orders' when committing atrocities during World War II. He sought to determine how far people would go in obeying authority, even when it conflicted with their personal morals.

Milgram's experiment involved paying male volunteers to participate. Each volunteer was paired with another person, with one assigned as the 'teacher' and the other as the 'learner'. The assignment was rigged so that the real participant was always the 'teacher', while the 'learner' was actually an actor.

The 'learner' was taken into a separate room, strapped to electrodes, and instructed to memorise word pairs. The 'teacher' sat in another room with an authority figure—a scientist in a white lab coat—who instructed them to administer electric shocks whenever the 'learner' made a mistake. The shocks increased in intensity with each incorrect answer, from a mild 15 volts to a dangerous 450 volts.

Unbeknownst to the 'teacher,' no actual shocks were given. However, the 'learner' pretended to be in increasing pain, eventually screaming and begging for mercy. If the 'teacher' hesitated or refused to continue, the authority figure issued firm commands to proceed.

Milgram's findings were shocking:

- All participants continued administering shocks up to 300 volts.
- 65% of participants obeyed until the maximum 450 volts.

Milgram repeated variations of the study 17 times, consistently reaching the same conclusion: obedience to authority is deeply ingrained in all of us, instilled from childhood through family, school, and the workplace. He summarised his findings by stating:

> *"The extreme willingness of adults to go to almost any lengths on the command of an authority constitutes the chief finding of the study."* [52]

This highlights how early programming makes us susceptible to unquestioningly following authority figures—even when doing so may be morally or legally questionable.

---

[52] McLeod, S. (2017) *The Milgram Shock Experiment. Simply Psychology.* www.simplypsychology.org/milgram.html

EXAMPLE: WHAT WOULD YOU DO?

Imagine your boss asks you to do something ethically dubious, if not outright illegal. Would you challenge her? Would you refuse? Would you report her? Or would you assume that, as an authority figure, she must know best? Would fear of losing your job lead you to comply without question?

This could explain how staff at companies like Enron and Arthur Andersen were complicit in corporate fraud. Enron, once a major US energy company, collapsed after it was discovered that it had used accounting tricks to hide billions of dollars in debt. Arthur Andersen, a global accounting firm, was found guilty of shredding documents to cover up Enron's fraud—ultimately leading to its downfall. [53] One could argue that blind obedience to authority played a role in this catastrophic corporate collapse.

We've seen this pattern throughout history, from extreme cases like Nazi Germany to everyday corruption in politics, where leaders abuse their power—whether by awarding government contracts to friends, violating lockdown laws, or accepting political donations in exchange for honours. This is why it's crucial to understand how your brain works. Engaging System 2 allows you to question authority and make more informed decisions.

Rewiring Your Programmes

While programmes are designed to help you adapt and navigate challenges, some eventually become limiting, leading to negative thought patterns, unhelpful feelings, and behaviours that hold you back. These deeply ingrained mental scripts—whether broad societal ideas (*'I must obey authority', 'The world is unsafe'*) or personal ones (*'I'm not good enough', 'I'm powerless'*)—often run on autopilot, shaping how we see ourselves and the world.

---

[53] *ABC News. 8 December 2009. Arthur Anderson goes out of business. https://abcnews.go.com/Business/Decade/arthur-andersen-business/story?id=9279255*

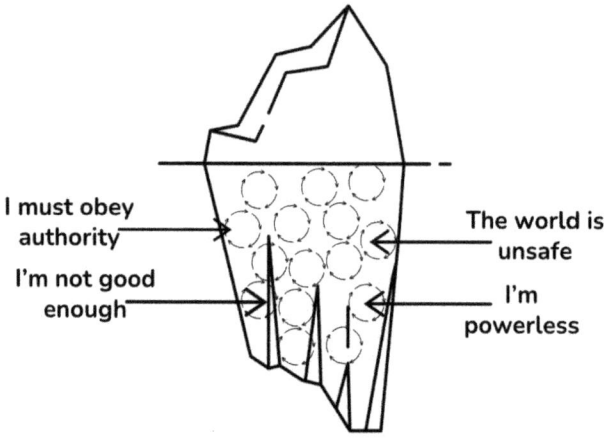

Nuances of The Success Cycle

Understanding the nature of your programming explains the nuances of the Success Cycle that were alluded to in Chapter 2, when Sam went for an interview. Sam thought she wouldn't get the job, yet was surprised when she did. At first glance, this seemed to contradict the Success Cycle, but her programming explains why it still applies.

> **EXAMPLE: SAM'S PROGRAMME**
>
> We know that Sam has a programme: '*I'm not good enough*'.[54] This programme explains why she thought she wouldn't get the job. However, she also had another programme that helped her cope with day-to-day life: '*I am capable if I can prepare fully*'. When faced with a job interview, her second programme kicks in and she prepares fully. As a result, Sam gets the job despite thinking that she won't: her preparation means that she comes across in the interview as someone who is knowledgeable and keen, and has a positive attitude.
>
> Yet, her '*I'm not good enough*' programme won't disappear. It may cause her to reject the job offer, fearing she wouldn't measure up. Or if she accepted it, she might overwork

---

[54] *In Activity 14 in Chapter 7 we learn that the reason Sam can't let go and move on when something goes wrong is because if she makes a mistake it means that she's not good enough.*

herself to avoid being 'exposed' as incompetent, leading to stress, burnout, and ultimately reinforcing her programme that she isn't good enough.

The good news? No matter how deeply ingrained they feel, you can replace them with different, more empowering programmes. How is this possible? By understanding what they *really* are.

11.07 What the Programmes Are

So… what are they?

At their core, these programmes are beliefs.

Beliefs are deeply held convictions, opinions, and attitudes that individuals accept as true. But here's the key: beliefs are not facts or universal truths—though your brain may treat them as such because of how it constructs your reality.

The critical difference between beliefs and facts is that beliefs are subjective and cannot always be universally proven. Facts, by contrast, are objective truths that can be verified.

Beliefs vs. Facts: An Example

A belief: *Walking under a ladder brings bad luck.*
A fact: *Water boils at 100°C at sea level.*

There's a practical reason why walking under a ladder might not be the best idea—it's a potential safety hazard. But does it *actually* cause bad luck? Not necessarily.

However, if someone believes it does, their brain will look for evidence to confirm that belief. If something goes wrong after they walk under a ladder, they'll attribute it to 'bad luck.' And if something good happens? They might dismiss it as a fluke.

On the other hand, another person might believe walking under a ladder brings good luck, noticing every positive event that follows and linking it to the act.

So, who's right? Both—because their belief shapes their experience. And neither—because belief is not the same as objective truth.

In contrast, facts remain constant. Water will always boil at 100°C at sea level, regardless of personal beliefs or interpretations. Unlike subjective beliefs, facts are universally observable and repeatable.

Now that you understand your programmes are simply beliefs, here's the best part: beliefs can be changed. While many of your beliefs support you and drive the Success Cycle in a positive direction, others work against you, steering it toward unwanted outcomes. These self-sabotaging beliefs hinder your progress and prevent you from achieving what you truly want. We won't alter the beliefs that serve you well, but we will focus on transforming those that hold you back. These are known as limiting beliefs.

11.08 How Change Is Possible

Your limiting beliefs may have existed for a long time, but that doesn't mean they're permanent. Why? Because beliefs are not the truth—they're an illusion. What's more, due to neuroplasticity (the concept you first encountered in Chapter 2) it is—physiologically—possible to change them.

Neuroplasticity means that your brain is not fixed—it is flexible. It continuously grows, learns, and rewires itself throughout your entire life. This means that changing your beliefs is possible—and history is full of proof.

> Before 1954, experts said that the human body was not capable of running a mile in four minutes or less. It was *believed* the human body couldn't physically go that fast because it would collapse under the exertion. On 6 May 1954, Sir Roger Bannister ran the first sub-four-minute-mile and proved the 'experts' wrong. What's more, once the belief had changed, the Australian Olympic track athlete

John Landy beat Bannister's time just forty six days later. Now, it's considered so normal that even strong high-school students can run a four-minute mile.[55]

How many people do you know who believe that they're 'past it' once they reach middle age? Remember that this is just a belief. It's not a truth. How do I know? Because there are amazing people who do remarkable things when they should be napping in front of the television (if you buy into the 'past it' belief that is).

> Consider the case of a Mexican Indian called Victoriano Churro, a farmer who belongs to a tribe called the Raramuri, and who won a race called the Leadville Trail 100. The Leadville Trail 100 is one of the most grueling marathons in North America because competitors have to run and climb 100 high-altitude miles over rough terrain and snowy peaks of the Colorado Rockies. The magazine *Runner's World* says that the race is closer to mountaineering than marathoning. In 1993, Churro won the race in a time of 20:03:33 when he was 55. Apparently, the Raramuri believe that runners reach their prime when they are approaching 60. Their positive belief led to a truly impressive reality![56]

Ultimately, it is possible to change beliefs.

Chapter Summary

As your brain is housed within your skull, it has to rely on the information it receives from the outside world via your five senses to determine what's actually going on around it. As a vast amount of data bombards your senses, your brain makes mental shortcuts to save time and energy, and it has a powerful filtering system to prevent information overload. Beliefs are one way in which information is

---

[55] Runyon, J. (2014). Impossible Case Study: Sir Roger Bannister and The Four-Minute Mile. Impossible. www.impossiblehq.com/impossible-case-study-sir-roger-bannister

[56] McDougall, C. (2018). Secrets of the Tarahumara. Runner's World. https://www.runnersworld.com/runners-stories/a20954821/born-to-run-secrets-of-the-tarahumara

filtered: your brain deletes, distorts, and generalises information from the outside world to fit what you believe.

Beliefs are so powerful that they drive what you expect to see. It's a natural part of being human. It's how our brains evolved to ensure our survival (something they've been very successful at doing to date!) In addition to being energy-efficient, our brains ensure that we can live our day-to-day lives without being overwhelmed (or unnecessarily bothered) by too much information.

Overall, our brains are amazing, and have enabled us to make technological advancements and create masterpieces in music, art, and literature. The problem is that, while beliefs help us to function effectively in the world, some beliefs become self-limiting and can hold you back from achieving professional success. The good news is that you're experiencing a *subjective* reality rather than an *objective* reality. So, when you change your beliefs on the inside, you automatically change your experience of reality on the outside.

What's Next?

You now have a fundamental understanding that internal beliefs are key to determining how you experience the 'reality' of your external world. In the next—and final—chapter, you'll discover how you can use self-coaching to identify and transform your limiting beliefs so that you can be confident, courageous and resilient without having to consciously and consistently make an effort.

12

CHANGE YOUR
CORE CONFIDENCE—PERMANENTLY

"If your beliefs are true then you have nothing to lose by subjecting them to scrutiny. If they are false, then you have everything to gain"
Peter Boghossain[57]

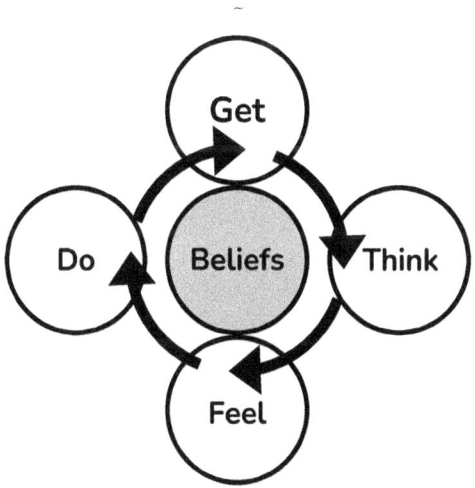

After reading the last chapter, Sam realises that the activities in Part Two have already revealed her limiting beliefs: I'm

---

[57] Peter Boghossian is an American philosopher and pedagogist.

incompetent, I'm incapable, and I'm not good enough. She also understands exactly where they originated.

She had a happy childhood with her parents and older brother, Ali, but she always felt like she wasn't as important as him; he seemed to be the focus of their mum and dad's attention. For example, Sam and Ali would spend hours climbing trees, swimming in the sea, and exploring the local woods on their bikes. But when they returned home, their parents would praise Ali for being clever and resourceful, listening intently as he explained their adventures.

Sam can't remember them even looking at her, let alone showing interest in her experience. Over time, she learned to avoid eye contact. The message she absorbed was clear: I'm not good enough. I'm not as important as Ali.

As they got older, the gap widened. Ali received even more love and attention whenever he achieved something great at school. He was so bright that their parents put him forward for a scholarship at a prestigious private school. When he was accepted, their dad took on extra shifts, and their mum got a part-time job to afford the fees—leaving them with even less time for Sam. Worse still, there was never any mention of putting her forward for a scholarship.

It would seem that, no matter how much effort she put in or how well she did at school, it was never enough. She never received the praise, recognition, or attention she longed for. But she did internalise a set of limiting beliefs.

Like Sam, you may have already identified some of your limiting beliefs and traced them back to their origins. You may also recognise how they shape your experiences at work. If you're not yet sure of your limiting beliefs, don't worry—that's exactly what this chapter will help you uncover.

You'll learn a step-by-step self-coaching process to identify, transform, and even rewire your limiting beliefs. You'll also explore a variety of techniques for shifting these beliefs, giving you multiple options to experiment with. Some methods may resonate more with you than others, and that's perfectly fine.

This journey will empower you to reshape how you make decisions, take action, and perceive yourself. As a result, you'll approach situations with greater confidence, assertiveness, courage, and resilience. By embracing this transformation, you'll cultivate a more positive and empowering reality—unlocking your full potential and laying a solid foundation for professional growth.

What This Chapter Covers:

- 12.01 Identifying Limiting Beliefs
- 12.02 Networks of Beliefs
- 12.03 The Root Cause of Beliefs
- 12.04 The Power of Identifying Your Limiting Beliefs
- 12.05 Seeking Contrary Evidence
- 12.06 Challenging Mental Filters
- 12.07 Practicing Belief-Challenging Techniques
- 12.08 Overcoming Limiting Beliefs
- 12.09 Rewiring Your Brain
- 12.10 A Shortcut to Success

12.01 Identifying Limiting Beliefs

Like Sam, you may have already gained some clarity about your limiting beliefs. If you haven't, don't worry—without realising it, you've already laid much of the groundwork in Part Two! Now, let's revisit some of the activities you completed and uncover what they revealed.

Assertiveness

In *Chapter 5—Activity 11 (Step 2)*, you reflected on the fears behind your non-assertive behaviour.

For example, Sam noted:

> "I avoid speaking to Muhammed and Belle for fear of confrontation. I'm mainly concerned that they'll think I'm not competent or capable."

Unknowingly, she had uncovered two limiting beliefs: "I'm not competent" and "I'm not capable." In order to engage in Mind Reading, she had to already believe these things about herself.

Courage

In *Chapter 7—Activity 14*, you examined the deeper meanings behind your self-sabotaging behaviours.

For example, Sam identified:

- Speaking up in meetings → *"I worry I might say something silly."*
- Promoting my strengths → *"If people expect too much from me, I might disappoint them."*
- Taking on new challenges → *"If I fail, people will think I'm an imposter."*
- Delivering last-minute presentations → *"If I don't prepare enough, people will think I'm not capable."*
- Letting go after mistakes → *"If I make a mistake, it means I'm not good enough."*

These statements revealed many of Sam's limiting beliefs, such as 'I'm not good enough', 'I'm not capable', 'I'm an imposter', 'I am a disappointment', and 'I am silly'. Again, to *mind-read* what others might think or assign meaning to these situations, Sam already had to hold these beliefs in System 1.

Resilience & Self-Talk

In *Chapter 10—Activity 20*, you explored the impact of self-talk by identifying Meta Model patterns.

For example, Sam's self-talk included:

- *"I can't switch off from work because I worry that Belle will think I'm incapable."*
- *"I can't do last-minute presentations because I'm scared they'll think I'm incompetent or not good enough."*

Once again, the same limiting beliefs—*'I'm incapable'* and *'I'm not good enough'*—surfaced.

Activity 22: Identify Your Limiting Beliefs

1. Review your past activities (*Chapter 5—Activity 11, Chapter 7—Activity 14, and Chapter 10—Activity 20*). Do they reveal limiting beliefs you weren't aware of at the time?
2. Look for patterns. Do your limiting beliefs share common themes?
3. Can you trace these beliefs back to a particular experience or time in your life?

12.02 Networks of Beliefs

As you identify your limiting beliefs, you may notice that many of them stem from a single, deeply rooted core belief. These core beliefs act like the foundation of a house, influencing a network of related thoughts, emotions, and behaviours.

Through years of research, training, and coaching, I've found that most limiting beliefs can be traced back to a few fundamental core beliefs:

- 'I'm not important.'
- 'I'm powerless.'

- 'I'm not valuable.'
- 'I'm not good enough.'
- 'I'm worthless.'

For example, Sam's limiting belief *'I'm not good enough'* isn't isolated—it branches into beliefs like *'I'm not capable', 'I'm an imposter'*, and *'I am silly'*. These, in turn, lead her to overwork, hesitate to speak up, or downplay her achievements.

If you've uncovered multiple limiting beliefs, ask yourself: Is there a common core belief behind them? Try mapping them out in a belief cascade diagram (as above) to see how they connect.

12.03 The Root Cause of Beliefs

As many of your limiting beliefs took root in childhood, they were likely shaped by the people who raised you. However, rather than falling into the trap of blame, consider this: the people who influenced your beliefs—parents, caregivers, siblings—were shaped by their own experiences too.

For example, if you struggle with intimacy and attribute it to your parents' divorce when you were five, ask yourself: *Could my parents have struggled with intimacy themselves?* Instead of focusing on blame, shift your perspective to focus on breaking the cycle.

You might find that some limiting beliefs stem from seemingly insignificant experiences—small, everyday moments that, at the time, felt unimportant.

> **For example**, I once worked with a delegate who spoke very quietly when nervous, almost to the point of being incomprehensible. When we explored why, he traced it back to a childhood habit: his mother worked from home, and he was constantly told, *"Shhh, your mum's working."* Though this was a simple instruction at the time, he had unconsciously carried it into adulthood, believing he needed to stay quiet and unnoticed.
>
> Once he recognised the connection, the belief instantly lost its power. He saw how irrational it was. As a result, his voice naturally became stronger and more confident.

Sometimes, limiting beliefs are a result of misunderstandings.

> **For example**, Sam had always felt that her parents favoured her brother, Ali—giving him more attention, encouragement, and opportunities. Eventually, she plucked up the courage to ask her mother why. To her shock, her mum was deeply upset that she had ever thought this. Her mother explained:
>
> Ali was a needy child who required constant reassurance, while Sam had always been so independent and capable that they trusted her to manage on her own.
>
> They had sent Ali to private school not because he was better, but because he had fallen in with the wrong crowd, and they feared for his future. They knew Sam would succeed no matter where she studied.
>
> This revelation shook Sam to the core. The belief that she wasn't good enough—one that had held her back for years—was based on a simple misunderstanding. It was

never true. Yet, it had unconsciously shaped her decisions, self-worth, and career confidence.

Exploring your past may stir strong emotions, and that's okay. Tears may come—not just from sadness, but from relief as you finally understand the roots of your thoughts, feelings, and behaviours.

However, if your exploration uncovers deeply painful or traumatic experiences, consider seeking professional support. A belief formed through trauma may require counselling or therapy to fully process and heal. The techniques in this course are powerful, but they are not designed to address unhealed trauma. Professional guidance is essential in such cases.

Whatever limiting beliefs you've discovered, remember: they are not facts. They are learned perspectives—meaning they can be unlearned and replaced with empowering beliefs.

12.04 The Marvel of Identifying Limiting Beliefs

Identifying and understanding your limiting beliefs can sometimes be enough to shift them. Even if they don't immediately change, you've taken a crucial step forward—moving your belief from System 1 (automatic thinking) to System 2 (conscious awareness), where you can actively challenge and reprogramme it.

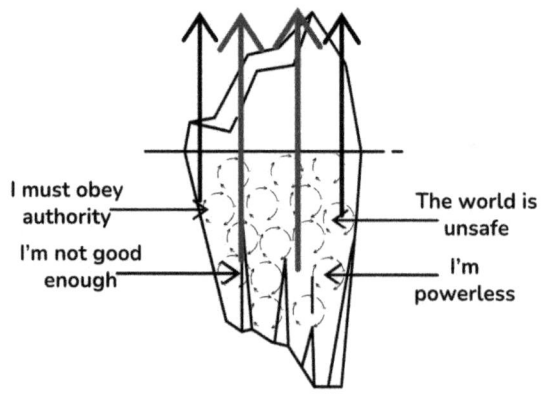

It's possible to challenge and reprogramme beliefs consciously

This is why all the work you've done so far has been so important. By bringing your limiting beliefs into your conscious awareness, you engage your Reticular Activating System (RAS)—the brain's filtering mechanism. Once activated, your RAS will start noticing new evidence that challenges your old belief, reshaping the way you interpret situations.

> **For example**, now that Sam recognises her belief that she's incapable without preparation, her RAS will start filtering experiences differently. Instead of automatically assuming she's unprepared and incompetent, she'll begin noticing moments where she succeeds despite little preparation. Likewise, if she previously hesitated to speak in meetings for fear of saying something silly, she may now choose to speak up—realising that it's unrealistic to always say something profound. Even if she uses a few filler words, instead of seeing it as evidence of incompetence, she may now view it as an opportunity to refine her communication skills.

By identifying and questioning her limiting beliefs, Sam disrupts her System 1's default assumptions. The same applies to you. Through previous exercises—such as reframing your thinking and challenging your self-talk—you've already begun loosening the grip of assumptions that reinforced your beliefs. This shift makes your brain more receptive to new possibilities, empowering you to rewrite your narrative and create a new reality.

12.05 Seeking Contrary Evidence

If awareness alone doesn't shift a belief, the next step is to actively seek evidence that contradicts it. You can:

- Ask for external input. Talk to someone you trust. They may highlight examples that disprove your belief.

- Do some research. Read articles, success stories, or studies that challenge your assumptions.

Some limiting beliefs are shaped by workplace culture or industry norms. For instance, many companies promote the idea that *climbing the corporate ladder defines success*. However, in creative fields or entrepreneurship, success is often measured by personal fulfilment, innovation, or work-life balance. To challenge a belief like this, explore different career paths, read interviews, and examine case studies of people who have achieved success in unconventional ways.

For example, Sam researches Imposter Syndrome and discovers an article, which states:

'Imposter syndrome is a persistent feeling of inadequacy despite evident success. Many high-achievers suffer from it, and it doesn't necessarily indicate low self-confidence. Researchers link it to perfectionism, especially in women and academics. Some believe it stems from childhood labels—for example, one sibling being 'the intelligent one' while another is 'the sensitive one'.'

Sam reflects:

"This makes so much sense! My brother Ali was always labelled as 'the intelligent one', while I was 'the sensible one'. No wonder I feel like I have to prove myself. The article suggests reminding myself that it's normal not to know everything and reframing thoughts like 'I'm incapable' into 'I may not be able to do this yet, but I can learn'."

By exposing herself to new perspectives, Sam begins to challenge her programmes.

Now, let's explore another self-coaching technique that will help you break free from limiting beliefs.

12.06 Challenging Mental Filters

In Chapter 10, you learned how System 1 filters reality through deletions, distortions, and generalisations. Now, you'll apply those skills to limiting beliefs, pushing even further. This process may feel uncomfortable, but the more uncomfortable it is, the deeper your transformation.

Let's examine Sam's belief: "If I don't have time to prepare a presentation, I am not capable."

1. **Question:** *"How does not having time to prepare mean I'm not capable?"*

   Answer: *"Because when I don't prepare, I mess up."*

Notice the missing logical connection ('means that'). Let's challenge this further:

2. **Question**: *"How does not preparing mean I will mess up?"*

   Answer: *"Being prepared means I know the topic well, sound authoritative, and can answer any question."*

Notice the missing logical connection again ('means that'). Let's challenge this further:

3. **Question:** *"Do I know people who are highly knowledgeable but don't come across as authoritative? Or people who aren't fully prepared but still seem confident?"*

   Answer: *"Yes! So, maybe it's not just about preparation."*

4. **Question**: *"Am I saying that if I'm not fully prepared, people will think I'm not good enough?"*

   Answer: *"Yes. I feel like I always have to prove that I'm good enough."*

At this point, Sam has a breakthrough:

> *"When I was a child, my brother got all the praise. I felt I had to prove that I was as good as my brother so that I could be loved and accepted as part of the family. But no matter how well I did, I was never noticed. So I decided to be as good as my brother. I would work longer and harder—eventually devising a secret strategy: waking up in the middle of the night to study. However, no matter how hard I worked, it wasn't enough—I*

wasn't good enough. I also felt like an imposter because I was trying to be someone I wasn't—my brother."

Like Sam, you may uncover deep insights about yourself through this process. It might feel challenging at first, but by systematically questioning your limiting beliefs, you can dismantle them and replace them with empowering perspectives.

To make this easier, the following exercise will help you to practice challenging your limiting beliefs, helping you refine this skill until it becomes second nature. The more you engage in this process, the more you'll develop the ability to shift your mindset and unlock new possibilities for growth and success.

12.07 Practicing Challenging Limiting Belief Filters

Let's put your self-coaching skills to the test by identifying limiting beliefs in common workplace scenarios and using questioning techniques to challenge them.

Activity 23: Workplace Scenario Practice

For each scenario below, identify the limiting belief and challenge it using self-coaching questions.

Scenario 1: Taking on Leadership Roles

- Desire: I want to take on more leadership roles.
- Obstacle: I don't think I have what it takes.
- Limiting Belief: 'I am not capable.'
- Challenge It:

Scenario 2: Speaking Up in Meetings

- Desire: I want to speak up when I disagree.
- Obstacle: I don't want to upset people.
- Limiting Belief: 'Disagreement equals conflict.'
- Challenge It:

Scenario 3: Networking More

- Desire: 'I want to network more.
- Obstacle: I feel like I have nothing valuable to say.
- Limiting Belief: 'I have nothing valuable to contribute.'
- Challenge It:

Scenario 4: Setting Boundaries with Colleague

- Desire: I want to set boundaries with colleagues.
- Obstacle: I don't want to be seen as difficult.
- Limiting Belief: 'Setting boundaries means being difficult.'
- Challenge It:

Scenario 5: Putting Myself Forward for New Opportunities

- Desire: I want to put myself forward for new opportunities.
- Obstacle: I'm not ready yet.
- Limiting Belief: 'I am not ready.'
- Challenge It:

Scenario 6: Negotiating Better Pay

- Desire: I want to negotiate better pay.
- Obstacle: I don't want to seem greedy.
- Limiting Belief: 'Asking for more means being greedy.'
- Challenge It:

Scenario 7: Taking More Career Risks

- Desire: I want to take more risks in my career.
- Obstacle: I don't want to make the wrong decision.
- Limiting Belief: 'A wrong decision will ruin everything.'
- Challenge It:

Scenario 8: Challenging Unfair Treatment

- Desire: I want to challenge unfair treatment.
- Obstacle: I don't want to create tension.
- Limiting Belief: 'Speaking up means creating conflict.'
- Challenge It:

Scenario 9: Feeling More Confident in Meetings

- Desire: I want to feel more confident in meetings.
- Obstacle: I'm afraid I'll say something dumb.
- Limiting Belief: 'Saying something wrong means looking foolish.
- Challenge It:

Scenario 10: Trusting My Team More

- Desire: I want to trust my team more.
- Obstacle: If I don't control everything, things will fall apart.
- Limiting Belief: 'Letting go means losing control.'
- Challenge It:

Spoiler Alert: Answers to Activity 23 below:

Scenario 1: Taking on Leadership Roles

- Challenge It:
  - What does 'having what it takes' actually mean?
  - What specific skills or experiences do I think I'm missing?

Scenario 2: Speaking Up in Meetings

- Challenge It:

- How does disagreeing automatically mean upsetting people?
- How do I know they'll be upset?

Scenario 3: Networking More

- Challenge It:
  - Nothing? Have I ever shared something useful before?
  - What does 'valuable' mean in this context?

Scenario 4: Setting Boundaries with Colleagues

- Challenge It:
  - Who specifically would see me as difficult?
  - How does setting a boundary automatically mean I'm being difficult?

Scenario 5: Putting Myself Forward for New Opportunities

- Challenge It:
  - What does 'ready' actually mean?
  - How is waiting helping me to become ready?

Scenario 6: Negotiating Better Pay

- Challenge It:
  - What specifically makes asking for fair compensation greedy?
  - When can negotiating actually be seen as professional or confident?

Scenario 7: Taking More Career Risks

- Challenge It:
  - How would a wrong decision ruin everything?
  - Everything? Are there any exceptions?

Scenario 8: Challenging Unfair Treatment

- Challenge It:
    - How does speaking up automatically create tension?
    - How do I know how others will react?

Scenario 9: Feeling More Confident in Meetings

- Challenge It:
    - What specifically makes a statement 'dumb'?
    - How does saying something wrong mean I'll look foolish?

Scenario 10: Trusting My Team More

- Challenge It:
    - What specifically will fall apart?
    - When has trusting others actually led to a positive result?

12.08 Challenging Your Limiting Beliefs

Now that you've practiced identifying and challenging limiting beliefs, it's time to apply self-coaching techniques to your own ones.

Activity 24: Self-Coaching Transformation

1. **Choose a Questioning Technique.**

    Select a questioning technique to challenge each limiting belief you've identified. Follow the conversation with yourself until you experience a shift in perspective.

    - **Simple Deletion**: Challenge what's missing or unclear by asking, "What specifically?"
    - **Complex Equivalence:** Challenge how two ideas are linked by asking, "How does X mean Y?"

- **Mind Reading:** Challenge assumptions about others' thoughts by asking, "How do I know that what they are thinking is true?"
- **Cause-Effect:** Challenge causal relationships by asking, "How specifically does X cause Y?"
- **Universal Quantifier:** Challenge absolutes (e.g., 'always', 'never') by asking, "Always? Are there exceptions?"
- **Nominalisation:** Turn an abstract noun into a verb and challenge it by asking, "How specifically?" or "According to whom?"
- **Comparative Deletion:** Challenge vague comparisons by asking, "Compared to what?"
- **Modal Operator of Necessity:** Challenge rules or obligations by asking, "What would happen if you didn't?" or "Who says you have to?"
- **Modal Operator of Possibility:** Challenge assumptions about what is or isn't possible by asking, "When is it possible?" or "How do you know it's impossible?"
- **Unspecified Verb:** Challenge vague actions by asking, "How specifically?" or "What specifically do you mean by that?"

2. **Reflect on Your Insights**

    Notice how these questions shift your perspective. How do they change the way you see your limiting beliefs?

If, like Sam, you find that identifying your limiting beliefs is not enough to change them, don't worry. System 1's programmes can be deeply ingrained, making it difficult to change them even when System 2 recognises that the belief is illogical. Sometimes, a limiting belief is so embedded that it needs to be reprogrammed with a new, empowering belief. To do this, we need to explore the science behind how beliefs are formed and changed—through neuroscience.

12.09 Rewiring Your Brain

Neural pathways are key to understanding how beliefs are formed—and how they can be changed. According to Brazilian neuroscientist Dr Suzana Herculano-Houzel, the human brain consists of approximately 86 billion neurons.[58]

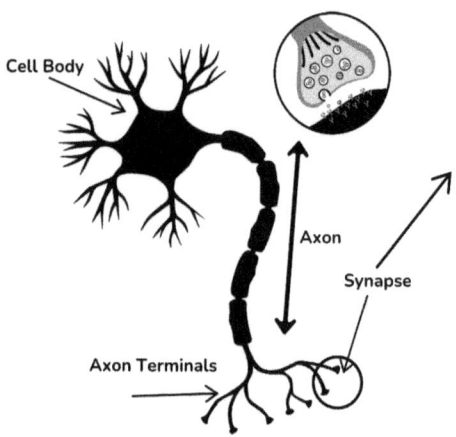

Neurons are the basic building blocks of the nervous system. A synapse is the small gap between two neurons across which signals pass from one to another. When you learn something new—whether a skill, habit, or belief—neurons fire together, creating neural pathways. The more a behaviour is repeated, the stronger its neural pathway becomes. This is how habits and thought patterns, including limiting beliefs, are formed.

Like a river carving the easiest route through a canyon, your brain follows the path of least resistance—the most well-travelled neural pathways.[59] This is why ingrained habits feel automatic.

---

[58] Cherry, K. (2020). *How many neurons are in the brain? Very Well Mind.* https://www.verywellmind.com/how-many-neurons-are-in-the-brain-2794889#

[59] UCL News. (2017). *Humans are hard wired to follow path of least resistance.* University College of London. https://www.ucl.ac.uk/news/2017/feb/humans-are-hard-wired-follow-path-least-resistance

There's a saying in neuroscience: 'Neurons that fire together, wire together'. The more a set of neurons fire in a specific pattern, the stronger the connection becomes. That's why your brain defaults to familiar habits, even when you consciously want to change them.

Imagine your brain as a tropical island covered in dense jungle. Your old limiting belief is represented by a clear, well-trodden path through that jungle—the easiest route your brain follows automatically.

This explains why self-sabotage happens. Suppose you're trying to speak up in meetings, but when the moment arrives, you stay silent. Even though your rational mind (System 2) knows you should contribute, your brain defaults to the entrenched pathway of staying quiet. The same principle explains why you might accidentally drive to your old house after moving—you're so used to the old route that your brain follows it automatically.

But just as old paths can become overgrown, new pathways can be created. By deliberately practicing a new belief, you can rewire your brain to make it the new default.

Creating a New Empowering Belief

Now that you've identified at least one limiting belief, it's time to replace it with an empowering one—a belief that supports the success you want.

At first, this new belief might not feel true, and that's okay. What matters is consciously choosing it and practicing it until it becomes second nature.

Activity 25: New Belief

1. What new positive belief would you like to replace your old limiting belief with?

    - Sometimes, it's as simple as flipping a negative statement into a positive one (e.g., *"I am not important"* → *"I am important"*).

- Other times, you may need to be more creative. For example, *"I am an imposter"* could become *"I deserve to be here"* or *"I am worthy."*

Activity 25 - Sam's Answer:

"I would like to replace my old core limiting belief, 'I am not good enough', with a new empowering belief: 'I am good enough'."

Now that you've chosen a new belief, the next step is to act as if it's already true.

By consistently behaving as though you are the person who holds this new belief, you reinforce the new neural pathway while weakening the old one.

This process is backed by neuroscience. Neuroplasticity—the brain's ability to rewire itself—means that the more you act in alignment with your new belief, the more automatic it becomes.

This is what's commonly known as 'faking it until you make it' (first introduced in Chapter 4). Research shows that acting confidently, for example, actually makes you *feel* more confident over time.

At first, stepping into a new belief might feel uncomfortable, but it gets easier with practice. That's why this book has guided you step-by-step—building your skills gradually before tackling more challenging mindset shifts.

To help reinforce your new belief, try modelling a role model. Observe how confident people behave, then mimic their posture, tone, and mindset. Practicing in front of a mirror can also help.

Each time you 'fake it', you are walking along your new neural pathway, making it stronger while allowing the old one to fade. Over time, the new belief becomes your brain's default mode—the path of least resistance. When that happens, the old limiting belief ceases to exist.

Activity 26: Practice

How can you apply this method to rewire your brain?

Activity 26 - Sam's Answer:

"To help reinforce my new belief ('I am good enough'), I will:

- Stand tall and pull my shoulders back as a physical representation of 'I am good enough'. This will help me feel and look confident.

- Maintain eye contact with others by reminding myself 'I am as good as them'.

- Continue to practice setting boundaries. If I feel that something is unfair, it's up to me to address it rather than taking it out on Davide!

- Share my views and opinions in meetings because my thoughts are as valuable as everyone else's. Even if I don't always contribute something groundbreaking, that doesn't mean what I've said is silly.

- Volunteer for tasks outside my comfort zone (for example, last-minute presentations) before I have a chance to overthink. If I start to worry, I'll remind myself that I am good enough and that failure is just my 'First Attempt In Learning'.

- Remind myself that struggling to keep on top of my workload doesn't mean I'm not good enough, incompetent, or incapable. Instead, I'll ask myself: Why am I struggling? Do I have too much on my plate? Should I delegate more? Upskill a team member? Plan better? Set clearer boundaries? Do I need new skills or knowledge? Does the team need additional resources?

- Be strict with my self-talk. If doubt creeps in, I'll remind myself that I am good enough."

By actively practicing your new belief, you're not just changing how you think—you're rewiring your brain to make it your new reality. The moment your new empowering belief becomes more entrenched than the old limiting belief is the moment it becomes your truth.

12.10 Short-Cut to Success

If what I've described in the previous sections sounds like a lot of hard work and conscious effort, you're probably right. (Or is that just a belief?!) Fortunately, there's a shortcut to creating new neural pathways—visualisation.

Visualisation is the process of imagining yourself performing a new skill, behaviour, belief, or outcome. Essentially, you mentally 'see' yourself acting *as if* in your mind's eye. It works because the brain does not distinguish between real and imagined experiences.

In *How Your Mind Can Heal Your Body*, David R. Hamilton shares a study comparing the brains of people who played a sequence of piano notes with those who merely imagined playing them. After five days of daily practice, both groups exhibited identical brain changes—about 30-40 times growth in the neural area connected to finger movement. Brain scans revealed no difference between those who had physically played the notes and those who had only visualised doing so.

The Soviets pioneered the use of visualisation for sports performance in the 1970s; today, it's a widely adopted technique among elite athletes. Jessica Ennis-Hill, Andy Murray, Missy Franklin, and Novak Djokovic have all used visualisation to enhance their performance.

Olympic judoka Kayla Harrison, who defended her Olympic title at the Rio 2016 Games, practiced visualisation daily. She described picturing herself winning: *"Every night I visualise myself winning the Olympics. I picture myself bombing the girl in the final, standing on the podium, watching the flag go up, feeling the gold medal around my neck, and hugging my coach."* She went on to win her second Olympic gold medal in the 78 kg category.

You, too, can harness the power of your imagination to strengthen your new empowering beliefs and achieve desired outcomes. Not only is it fun, but it's also easy, free, and accessible anytime, anywhere.

How to Use Visualisation:

1. **Define your desired outcome:** Be clear about the new belief and the results you want.

2. **Create a vivid mental picture**: Imagine yourself living as if your new belief were already true.

    - **Engage all five senses:** What do you see? Who is with you? How do you feel? What are you saying to yourself? Are there specific sounds, tastes, or scents associated with the moment?
    - Ensure that the visualisation is positive, empowering, and emotionally compelling.

3. **Repeat daily**: Reinforce the belief through regular practice.

    - Ideally, visualise for at least one minute both when you wake up and before bed.
    - The more frequently and vividly you visualise, the stronger your new neural pathways become.

How Long Does It Take?

According to a study by Phillippa Lally, a health psychology researcher at University College London, it takes an average of 66 days to form a new habit. Her research tracked the habits of 96 participants over 12 weeks. While some habits took as little as 18 days to become automatic, others required up to 254 days, with 66 days as the average.[60]

While 66 days might seem long, the benefit is that once the new belief is ingrained, it becomes second nature. With consistent visualisation—just one minute, twice a day—you could establish a new belief in just over a month!

Activity 27: Final Action Plan

It's time to create a concrete action plan to reprogramme your limiting beliefs so that your programmes in System 1 work for you rather than

---

[60] Lally, P. (2010). *How are habits formed: Modelling habit formation in the real world. European Journal of Social Psychology.* https://onlinelibrary.wiley.com/doi/abs/10.1002/ejsp.674

against you. Revisit the objectives you identified in Activity 3 (Chapter 2) and apply what you've learned to solidify your transformation.

Step 1: Identify the Limiting Belief

- For each of your objectives, uncover the limiting belief that has been holding you back.
- Example: *"I'm not good enough to lead a project."*

Step 2: Replace It with an Empowering Belief

- Craft a new belief that supports your success.
- Example: *"I have the skills and knowledge to lead effectively."*

Step 3: Align Your Success Cycle with Your New Belief

- Identify specific thoughts, feelings and behaviours that reinforce your new belief.
- Example: If your belief is *"I am confident,"* act as if it's true:
  - Speak up in meetings.
  - Set boundaries assertively.
  - Use strong, deliberate body language.
  - Feel like a confident person (powerful, in control)
  - Think confident thoughts ("I am valuable"; "I am good enough.")

Step 4: Visualise Your Success

- Imagine yourself fully embodying this belief.
- Engage all your senses—how do you look, feel, and act in this new belief?
- Picture positive outcomes, reinforcing your new reality.

Step 5: Track Progress and Adjust

- Set measurable milestones (e.g., speak up in three meetings).
- Keep a journal or use an app to track your actions and results.
- Reflect weekly:
  - What progress have I made?
  - What challenges have I encountered?
  - How can I adjust my approach?

By consistently aligning your thoughts, actions, and emotions with your new belief, you'll rewire your brain for success.

Activity 27 - Sam's Answer:

1. My Limiting Belief

"I am not good enough." This belief made me feel like an imposter, doubt my abilities, and hold myself back in my career.

2. My New Empowering Belief

"I am good enough, capable, and deserving of success."

3. Actions to Reinforce My New Belief

To embed this belief into my daily life, I will:

- Demonstrate confidence physically by standing tall, keeping my shoulders back, and making eye contact in conversations.
- Speak with authority by replacing filler words ('um' and 'er') with intentional pauses.
- Set firm boundaries and remind myself that my time and opinions are just as valuable as anyone else's.

- Step outside my comfort zone by volunteering for new challenges, including last-minute presentations.
- Challenge negative self-talk by actively shutting down thoughts of self-doubt and reframing mistakes as learning opportunities.
- Stop assuming what others think and, instead, ask for clarity rather than jumping to conclusions.

4. Expected Results

By consistently practicing these actions, I expect to see the following changes:

- I will feel more comfortable speaking in meetings and taking on leadership roles.
- I will no longer over-prepare out of fear of being 'found out'.
- I will trust in my ability to handle challenges rather than fearing failure.
- I will gain more recognition for my contributions, positioning myself for career growth.
- I will feel more relaxed, sleep better, and have greater work-life balance.

5. My Progress So Far

I recently delivered a last-minute presentation to my team. While I initially felt nervous, it wasn't the catastrophe I had imagined. In fact, it was a positive experience that boosted my confidence. Now, I feel much less apprehensive about doing it again, knowing that practice will only make me better.

Belle even commented that I seem more confident and authoritative: she believes I'm on track for a promotion next year.

Most importantly, this shift hasn't just changed my career—it's transforming my entire life. I'm more at ease, more present in my personal life, and finally making time for things I enjoy.

Final Thought

This is more than just an exercise; it's a long-term commitment to becoming the person I know I can be. Every time I act in alignment with my new belief, I reinforce it, making it stronger than the limiting belief I left behind. I am ready to move forward with confidence.

By consistently practicing visualisation, you reinforce new neural pathways, making your empowering beliefs a permanent reality.

Chapter Summary

Throughout your journey through this book, you've uncovered the hidden beliefs that have been silently steering your professional life—beliefs that have fuelled self-sabotage and held you back from stepping into your most confident, assertive, courageous, and resilient self. Many of these beliefs took root in childhood, born from misunderstandings, fleeting moments, or even minor mistakes. Now, you know the truth: they were never facts—just stories your mind accepted as reality. And because they were created in an instant, some can dissolve just as quickly.

For deeper-rooted beliefs, you've learned how to reprogramme your mind by gathering counter-evidence, dismantling false assumptions, and asking powerful, challenging questions. Even the most stubborn beliefs crumble under the weight of truth.

But awareness alone isn't enough—you must take action. Neuroscience is on your side. You now understand how to rewire your brain by choosing an empowering belief, embracing it, and embodying it until it becomes second nature. It takes just 66 days to build new neural pathways—but with the power of visualisation, you can accelerate the process and step into your transformation even faster.

What's Next?

You've reached the final pages of this book, but this isn't the end. This is the beginning of a life without self-sabotage. You now hold an entire arsenal of tools to rewrite your narrative, break free from limitations, and step into the most unstoppable version of yourself.

Like an old pair of pyjamas that no longer fit, your limiting beliefs have served their time. It's time to let them go. Why hold on to something that no longer serves you?

Remember this: You are limitless. You have the power to shape your reality—to create instead of complain, to build instead of wish. The life you want isn't out of reach; it's waiting for you to claim it.

If you're not yet as confident, assertive, courageous, and resilient as you want to be—or if you're not yet achieving mind-blowing success—the only thing standing in your way is you. And the only person who can change that? You.

So go out there. Take action. Be bold. Reclaim your power. The future you desire is yours to create.

I will leave you with a powerful metaphor:

A business executive was deep in debt and could see no way out. Creditors were closing in on him and suppliers were demanding payment. He sat on the park bench, head in hands, wondering if anything could save his company from bankruptcy. Suddenly an old man appeared before him. "I can see that something is troubling you," he said. After listening to the executive's woes, the old man said, "I believe I can help you." He asked the man his name, wrote out a cheque, and pushed it into his hand saying, "Take this money. Meet me here exactly one year from today, and you can pay me back at that time." Then he turned and disappeared as quickly as he had come.

The business executive saw in his hand a cheque for $500,000, signed by John D. Rockefeller, then one of the richest men in the world! "I can erase my money worries in an instant!" he realised. But instead, the executive decided to put the uncashed cheque in his safe. Just knowing it was there might give him the strength to work out a way to save his business, he thought.

With renewed optimism, he negotiated better deals and extended terms of payment. He closed several big sales. Within a few months, he was out of debt and making money once again. Exactly one year later, he returned to the park with the uncashed cheque. At the agreed-upon time, the old man appeared. But just as the executive was about to hand back the cheque and share his success story, a nurse came running up and grabbed the old man. "I'm so glad I caught him!" she cried. "I hope he hasn't been bothering you. He's always escaping from the rest home and telling people he's John D. Rockefeller." And she led the old man away by the arm. The astonished executive just stood there, stunned. All year long he'd been wheeling and dealing, buying and selling, convinced he had half a million dollars behind him.

Suddenly, he realised that it wasn't the money, real or imagined, that had turned his life around. It was his newfound self-confidence that gave him the power to achieve anything he went after.[61]

---

[61] *A short story on self-confidence. (2013) Academic Tips.* https://www.academictips.org/blogs/a-short-story-on-self-confidence

ABOUT THE AUTHOR

If you'd met me in my twenties, you'd have thought I was confident and successful. On the outside, I had it all. But on the inside? I was drowning in self-doubt, anxiety, and a crushing sense that I just wasn't good enough. I was shy, suffered from panic attacks, and dreaded public speaking so much that I'd rather have done just about anything else—including jumping off a cliff.

While others seemed to thrive, I felt stuck. So I made it my mission to figure out what I was missing. I dived deep into anything that could help—Neuro-Linguistic Programming (NLP), Hypnosis, Cognitive Behavioural Therapy (CBT), and more. Over time, I rewired my thinking. And as my thoughts changed, so did everything else—my confidence, career, and overall happiness.

Ironically, the thing I once feared most—public speaking—became my greatest passion. Since then, I've spent over 20 years in Learning and Development, training and coaching thousands of professionals to build confidence, break through mental barriers, and unlock their full potential. In 2007, I launched my own business to focus on the mindset and soft skills that drive real success, and in 2017, I even published a saucy self-help novel called Blokes, Beers & Burritos!

In The Confidence Breakthrough, I bring together my personal journey and professional expertise to guide you through practical, neuroscience-backed strategies for lasting change. My philosophy is simple: professional success starts with personal transformation.

If this book helped you, I'd be truly grateful if you could take a moment to leave a review on Amazon. As an independently published author, I don't have a huge marketing team behind me—just readers like you who help spread the word. Your review can make a big difference. Thank you!

Want to Go Deeper?

If you'd like to deep your momentum going, I have two powerful resources to support your journey:

The Confidence Breakthrough Online Course

A six-month, video-based programme packed with mindset strategies, self-coaching tools, and behavioural techniques to accelerate your transformation. Work at your own pace and revisit lessons whenever you need a boost in confidence, courage, or resilience.

The Confidence Breakthrough Cards

A beautifully designed deck for daily reflection and motivation. Simply shuffle, pull a card, and use it to guide your next step. Ideal for staying grounded and focused—especially during moments of doubt.

Find out more at joblakeleytraining.co.uk

ACKNOWLEDGEMENTS

First and foremost, my deepest gratitude goes to Matt and Milo. Their unwavering encouragement and support were instrumental in bringing this book from my mind to the page. Their patience throughout the many frustrating stages of writing and rewriting has been invaluable. Without them, this book would not have been possible.

A special thank you to Jonathan Crowe[62] for his continuous support, brilliant insights, and expert editing. Looking back at the first manuscript I sent him five years ago (!), it was a sprawling, 100,000-word jumble—without structure, focus, or clear direction. Jonathan's exceptional ability to reshape and refine my work, his thoughtful suggestions, and his gentle yet constructive challenges pushed me to improve the book in ways I never could have done alone. I am truly grateful for his patience, kindness, and the steadfast support he has shown me over the years.

I would also like to thank Dr Stephen Cutler for his invaluable contributions to the direction of the book, particularly his brilliant suggestion to incorporate a fictional character to bring the concepts to life. This idea has significantly shaped the narrative in ways I hadn't imagined, and I'm thankful for his creativity and insight.

---

[62] https://www.linkedin.com/in/crowe-jon-309587/

Finally, a heartfelt thank you to Indie Authors World. Their dedication and professionalism have been immeasurable. They have turned my 65,000 word manuscript into the polished reality you now hold in your hands.

BIBLIOGRAPHY

Andreatta, Britt: Wired To Grow. 7th Mind Publishing. 2016

Bandler, Richard: *Using Your Brain*. Real People Press. 1985

Ben-Shahar, Tal: *Happier*. McGraw Hill. 2007

Branden, Nathaniel: *Six Pillars of Self-Esteem*. Bantam Press. 1995

Chabris, Christopher & Simons, Daniel: *The Invisible Gorilla*. Harper Collins 2011

Covey, Stephen: *The Seven Habits of Highly Effective People*. Simon and Schuster 2004

Chirimuuta, Dr Mazviita: *Outside Color: Perceptual Science and the Puzzle of Color in Philosophy*. MIT Press; Reprint edition 2017

Clear, James: Atomic Habits. Penguin Random House UK 2018

Darwin, Charles: Penguin Classics; *The Expression of the Emotions in Man and Animals*. Original edition 2009

Dispenza, Dr Joe: *Breaking The Habit of Being Yourself*. Hay House UK 2012

Dolan, Prof Paul: *Happiness By Design*. Penguin 2015

Duhigg, Charles: *The Power of Habit*. Random House Books 2013

Dweck, Carol: *Mindset*. Ballantine Books 213

Eagleman, David: *The Brain*. Canongate Books Ltd. 2015

Frankl, Vicktor: *Man's Search For Meaning*. Rider, New Ed edition 2004

Grinder, John & Bandler, Richard: *The Structure of Magic Volume I*. Science and Behaviour Books, Inc 1975

Grinder, John & Bandler, Richard: *The Structure of Magic Volume II*. Science and Behaviour Books, Inc 1976

Groves, Barry: *Trick and Treat*. Hammersmith Press Ltd. 2008

Hamilton, David R: *I Heart Me*. Hay House UK 2015

Hamilton, David R: *How Your Mind Can Heal Your Body*. Hay House UK 2008

Heffernan, Margaret: *Wilful Blindness*. Simon & Schuster UK Reissue edition 2011

Helmstetter, Shad: *What To Say When You Talk To Your Self*. Thorsons 1986

Hill, Napoleon: *The Law of Success*. Wilder Publications. 2011

Hill, Napoleon: *Think and Grow Rich*. Mindpower Press. Revised edition 2015

Jeffers, Susan: *Feel the Fear and Do It Anyway*. Vermillion. Revised edition 2007

Johnson, Rex & Swindley, David: *Awaken Your Inner Power*. Element Books. 1997

Kahneman, Daniel: *Thinking Fast and Slow*. Penguin 2012

Kahneman, Daniel: *Heuristics and Biases – The Psychology of Intuitive judgement*. Cambridge University Press 2002

Kiyosaki, Robert T: *Rich Dad, Poor Dad*. Plata Publishing 2011

Koga, Fumitake and Kishima, Ichiro: *The Courage to be Disliked*. Allen & Unwin; Main edition 2019

Kübler-Ross, Elizabeth: *On Death and Dying*. Scribner Book Company; Reprint edition (2014)

Lewis, Dr Jack & Webster, Adrian: *Sort Your Brain Out*. Capstone. 2014

Lipton, Bruce: *The Biology of Belief*. Elite Books. 2005

MacLean, Paul *The Triune Brain in Evolution*. Springer 1990th edition. 1990

Maister, David: *The Trusted Advisor*. Simon & Schuster UK; Reprint edition. 2002

Massey, Morris: *Puzzle People – Understanding Yourself*. Brady. 1979

Mehrabian, Albert: Silent Messages: Implicit Communication of Emotions and Attitudes . Wadsworth Publishing. 1972

McKay, Matthew & Fanning, Patrick: *Self-Esteem*. New Harbinger Publications. 1987

McKenna, Paul: *Change Your Life in 7 Days*. Bantam Press. 2004

McTaggart, Lynne: *The Field*. Harper Collins. 2003

Murphy, Joseph: *The Power of Your Subconscious Mind*. Parker Publishing. 1988

Owen, Nick: The Magic of Metaphor. Crown House Publishing Ltd. 2001

Perlmutter, David & Villoldo, Alberto: *Power Up Your Brain*. Hay House. 2011

Ready, Romilla & Burton, Kate: *Neuro-Linguistic Programming for Dummies*. John Wiley & Sons. 2004

Reynolds, Siimon: *Why People Fail*. Jossey-Bass. 2012

Robbins, Anthony: *Unlimited Power*. Simon & Schuster UK. 2001

Steinberg, Scott: *Make Change Work for You*. Piatkus. 2015

Taylor-Bolte, Jill: *My Stroke of Insight*. Hodder Paperbacks. 2009

Thomson, David: Political Ideas. Penguin Books. 1966

Todorov, Alexander: *Face Value*. Princeton University Press 2017

Newburg, Andrew & Waldman, Mark Robert: *Words Can Change Your Brain*. Penguin; Reprint edition 2014

www.ingramcontent.com/pod-product-compliance
Lighting Source LLC
Chambersburg PA
CBHW051558010526
44118CB00023B/2738